W9-AVH-756

Flying Fox
Applying Visual FoxPro Reporting to Any Data, in Any Enviroment

Lisa Slater Nicholls

ISYS Software- und Verlagsgesellschaft mbH
Frankfurter Str. 21 b, 61476 Kronberg, Germany
Copyright © 2006 by dFPUG c/o ISYS GmbH

Published by:
> ISYS Softwareentwicklungs- und Verlagsgesellschaft mbH
> Frankfurter Str. 21 b, 61476 Kronberg, Germany

By ISYS GmbH published books are available through booksellers and directly from the publisher. Contact ISYS Softwareentwicklungs- und Verlagsgesellschaft mbH :
> Tel. 0049-6173-950903, Fax 0049-6173-950904
> www.dFPUG.de, Redaktion@dFPUG.de

Visual FoxPro® 9.0 Reporting With External Data
> By Lisa Slater Nicholls
> Technical Edidor: Colin Malcolm Nicholls
> Cover: Kent Gerber

ISBN No: 3-937133-09-7
Printed in Germany 2006

Chapter list

Flying Fox Applying Visual FoxPro Reporting to Any Data, in Any Enviroment I
Chapter list..III
Table of Contents V
Acknowledgements...VII
About the author IX
How to Download the Files...XI
Introduction XIII
Chapter 1 Prepare your development environment 1
Chapter 2 Bring your data into Visual FoxPro 3
Chapter 3 Create reports... 9
Chapter 4 Customize your report layouts.. 23
Chapter 5 Communicate complex data.. 35
Chapter 6 Use objects to make the process repeatable.. 71
Chapter 7 Create a VFP reporting application 99
Go forth and get output results!.. 141

Table of Contents

Flying Fox Applying Visual FoxPro Reporting to Any Data, in Any Enviroment I
Chapter list...III
Table of Contents V
Acknowledgements... VII
About the author IX
   Lisa Slater Nicholls IX
How to Download the Files...XI
Introduction XIII
   Who should read this book.. XIII
   Why VFP? XIII
   How to read this book XIV
   Icons and special notes.. XV
Chapter 1 Prepare your development environment 1
Chapter 2 Bring your data into Visual FoxPro 3
Chapter 3 Create reports... 9
   3.1 Adjust the VFP IDE 9
   3.2 Open the VFP Report Designer... 10
   3.3 Add data instructions to the report 10
   3.4 Save and run the report... 18
   3.5 Improve your Data Environment settings 19
Chapter 4 Customize your report layouts... 23
   4.1 Quick-start report designs 23
   4.2 Load the Data Environment from a similar report....................................... 25
   4.3 Test-run the report and its data-handling 27
   4.4 Customize your report layout elements.. 27
   4.5 Use Print When to print expressions selectively 29
   4.6 Repeat, and refine, your layout customizations 31
   4.7 Decide when to use Visual FoxPro expressions... 32
Chapter 5 Communicate complex data... 35
   5.1 Show data groups 35
   5.2 Handle multiple tables from your database.. 39
   5.3 Relate multiple cursors in the VFP environment 43
   5.4 Relate from the child to the parent 48
   5.5 Use multiple cursors in a VFP report... 49
   5.6 Use multiple detail bands for multiple parent-child relationships 55
   5.7 Use multiple detail bands without data relationships.................................. 64
   5.8 Move on to improving the process.. 69
Chapter 6 Use objects to make the process repeatable.............................. 71
   6.1 Introducing your first VFP class library.. 72
   6.2 Adding your VFP DataEnvironment class' data-intelligence to a report 74
   6.3 Introducing a generic VFP Class Library for Reporting............................... 78
   6.4 Running the report with your DataEnvironment.. 92
   6.5 Moving on to a VFP reporting application... 98
Chapter 7 Create a VFP reporting application 99
   7.1 Introducing the _frxcommand object 100
   7.2 Building a VFP reporting solution 101
   7.3 Deploying your VFP reporting application 107
   7.4 Understanding and preparing XML command files for _frxcommand........ 112
   7.5 Providing end-user design sessions using _frxcommand and PROTECTED reports.. 124
   7.6 Extending _frxcommand 128

7.7 Building a distributable VFP reporting solution 131
7.8 Some ideas and thoughts about invoking your VFP component in external applications
.... 138
Go forth and get output results!.. 141

Acknowledgements

The contents of this tutorial were inspired by, and are dedicated to, Rainer Becker. Businesses create databases because they want results, not because they want data, and Rainer believes, as I do, that Visual FoxPro provides unmatched tools for moving data into effective results (output). Rainer's faith in VFP's attractiveness as a tool for reporting, for database developers in any environment with any data, not to mention his personal powers of persuasion, are just as responsible for this book as is my own work.

As Rainer has publicly stated, "In my career, success has always been a sign of good craftsmanship and benefit to the customers. And in my view, the most profound success lies not only in good results in one's work life, but in managing to be a family man as well." My husband and co-developer, Colin Nicholls, and I have personal experience of Rainer's dedication to these balanced goals.

While there is great satisfaction in one's own internal awareness of working to high standards, success is also defined by external respect and acknowledgement of one's work. Rainer deserves respect and acknowledgement for his data- and business- intelligence, and also for his enthusiastic nurturing of VFP talent and techniques throughout the years. This book is only one result of many.

This document would also not exist without the creative partnership of Richard Stanton and Colin Nicholls throughout the VFP 9 development cycle, as we bounced ideas around in a joyous effort to scrutinize everything, reject nothing, and assimilate anything that would open up the VFP reporting universe. I hope that when they read my recommendations and reporting directions herein, they think to themselves, "didn't it clean up shiny!"

Colin has, of course, already read this book; otherwise it would make much less sense. A final, grateful, and hearty "thank you" to Colin and also to John O'Duffy, for much-needed reality checks at critical points in the writing process.

About the author

Lisa Slater Nicholls

Lisa Slater Nicholls is an independent software developer. She and Colin Nicholls provide enterprise data integration and analysis services using Visual FoxPro and XML in a variety of environments and languages (dba Spacefold). She has served in project management, design, and Xbase development roles for Visual FoxPro 9.0's report system features. She served as an integration engineer for Acxiom Corporation for four years, designing solutions for Oracle, Siebel, IBM, and other Acxiom Alliance partners.

Lisa has a special interest in the development of peer-to-peer support mechanisms in the programming community and was one of the original Microsoft Most Valuable Professionals. She has taught numerous FoxPro-RAD seminars and has been a featured speaker at major FoxPro and database conferences throughout the world. She served as editor of Pinnacle Publishing's *FoxTalk* journal and writer for various FoxPro and database development magazines. She was lead writer for the bestselling *Using FoxPro 2.x* volumes (Que) and *FoxPro MAChete* (Hayden), the author of the Report Writer volume of *Pros Talk Fox Series One*, and Series Editor for *Pros Talk Fox Series Two* (Pinnacle).

E-Mail: mailto:lisa@spacefold.com..

How to Download the Files

There are two sets of files that accompany this book. The first is the source code referenced throughout the text, and the second is the e-book version of this book—(.PDF) file. Here's how to get them.

Both the source code and the PDF file are available for download from the Hentzenwerke Web site. In order to obtain them, follow these instructions:

1. Point your Web browser to www.hentzenwerke.com.

2. Look for the link that says "Download Source Code." (The text for this link may change over time—if it does, look for a link that references Books or Downloads.)

3. A page describing the download process will appear.

This page has two sections:

- Section 1: If you were issued a username/password from Hentzenwerke Publishing, you can enter them into this page.

- Section 2: If you did not receive a username/password from Hentzenwerke don't worry! Just enter your e-mail alias and look for the question about your book. Note that you'll need your book when you answer the question.

4. A page that lists the hyperlinks for the appropriate downloads will appear.

Note that the .PDF file is covered by the same copyright laws as the printed book. Reproduction and/or distribution of the .PDF file is against the law.

If you have questions or problems, the fastest way to get a response is to e-mail us at books@hentzenwerke.com.

If you bought the book of a member of the FoxPro User Group of German language you have access to the book directory with source code and eBook at http://portaladmin.dFPUG.de via your normal portal login.

The eBook and printed copy are available at:

http://shop.dFPUG.com,

http://shop.dFPUG.de or

http://www.hentzenwerke.com.

Introduction

This book gives you the tools and techniques you need to use Visual FoxPro 9.0 for reporting applications, no matter what type of database you use and no matter what type of programmer you are.

Who should read this book

Database developers who have never used Visual FoxPro can use this book to learn how to use VFP as a low-cost and full-featured reporting tool for their data sources. VFP developers can read this book to take a fresh look at reporting strategies that make use of features new in VFP 9, with a comprehensive strategy for using external data with reports.

Why VFP?

Visual FoxPro provides a great way to provide reports for your applications. Even if you don't use FoxPro for anything else, VFP makes reporting accessible, extensible, and cost-effective:

- VFP reports use any kind of data source that can be accessed through ODBC or OLE-DB.

- VFP allows you to manipulate your data efficiently, with a minimum of programming, as part of report preparation.

- When you, as a developer, ship VFP reports (FRX files) as part of your applications, you can include the customizable Report Designer, so your end-users can personalize the output.

- The VFP components you distribute to run reports in your applications, and even the Report Designer components you can optionally provide for your users, are royalty-free.

In this document, you'll learn to access MySQL data in Visual FoxPro and create reports with that data. I will provide some recommendations suitable for using external data of any type in VFP reports. I will demonstrate using some custom-built VFP tools to help you standardize common tasks for multiple reports, which are part of the source code for this tutorial.

> *I'll use the standard MySQL World sample database in all my examples. You'll find the full world.sql script to create this database in the source code for this document, in the "prepare_data" subfolder. You can learn more about the World sample database at http://dev.mysql.com/doc/world-setup.html.*

If you don't use MySQL, you can follow along with the examples in Microsoft SQL Server. I have prepared a separate file, msworld.sql, which you can use to load the World database into your instance of MS SQL Server. Change the CREATE DATABASE statement at the top of the msworld.sql file to include appropriate paths for both the database and database log files on your system.

If you use other ODBC-compliant database servers, you should be able to edit the msworld.sql script slightly for their use as well.

How to read this book

This tutorial does not assume any previous VFP knowledge. If you are not currently a VFP developer, start at the first, brief chapter *(Prepare your development environment)* and read straight through to the last chapter, at whatever rate feels comfortable to you. At the beginning, you will learn to access your data interactively and easily in the Visual FoxPro development environment. In the middle, you will learn about VFP report construction and applying VFP object-oriented design techniques to reports. By the end, you will be delivering and deploying polished reporting applications.

If you are already a VFP user, you don't need help learning to use the VFP IDE, so you can begin in chapter 2 *(Bring your data into Visual FoxPro)*. If you've been using external data for a long time, you may be tempted to skip chapter 2 as well, but give it a quick skim first. You may find some of the book's recommendations for data use with reports to be a little different from what you use in your current VFP applications, and chapter 2's introductory instructions will let you know what to expect.

> *The book's approach to data access is tuned for a reporting-centric use of external data, in cases where little or no application-specific Visual FoxPro code should be expected to surround the generation of report output. For this reason, the instructions bind the data closely to reports. They also emphasize retrieval of large, read-only data sets, as is appropriate for reporting applications.*
>
> *You can substitute any VFP data-handling mechanism that you prefer after you review this section of the book.*

Non-VFP developers and VFP developers who are not experienced with reports can use chapters 3 *(Create reports)* and 4 *(Customize your report layouts)* as a basic course in report design. VFP developers experienced with reports can review chapter 3 briefly its recommendations on data access techniques (sections "Add data instructions to the report" and "Improve your data environment Settings"), and check chapter 4 for any layout tips and tricks that may be new to them in VFP 9.

Chapter 5 *(Communicate complex data)* describes the use of multiple tables in reports, a sophisticated "dance" with new and subtle steps in VFP 9, thanks to the introduction of multiple detail bands for report layouts. This chapter is for everybody, since it considers various and typical external data scenarios and how best to express them in output using VFP reporting tools. Use this chapter to organize and classify your data scenarios, and to identify appropriate data presentations for each.

Chapter 6 *(Use objects to make the process repeatable)* brings VFP's considerable OOP (object oriented programming) muscle into the reporting process. You learn to use VFP's DataEnvironment container class and its member object types, such as cursor adapters, in ways especially suitable to VFP reporting with external data. This chapter employs some techniques new in VFP 9. Beyond that, this section and the associated class library abstracts the data-handling recommendations you've learned about interactively in the earlier chapters, making them available to any application.

Finally, chapter 7 *(Create a VFP reporting application)* gives you a generic object and a application framework that will run your reporting commands in an end-user environment. You customize the framework for various applications by adding DataEnvironment subclasses that are knowledgeable about your data sources. For deployment, you add the reports you've created plus an XML configuration file specifying these reports and other conditions (such as whether end-users have the ability to modify reports or create new ones). Non-VFP developers will see exactly how to add these classes, build a VFP executable, and create an installable package in this chapter. Experienced VFP developers may enjoy using this build-and-go approach to include external reporting add-ons packages with their existing applications or, alternatively, deploy the generic _frxcommand object and its associated XML configuration file within their standard application strategy.

Icons and special notes

I use the following Icons to help you identify some types of special comments and notes in this book:

> *This icon means the associated note is a slight digression from the tutorial instructions in the current section of the book. It enriches your general knowledge of the current subject, but is not required to follow the tutorial to a successful conclusion.*

> *This icon means the associated comment is of special interest to experienced VFP developers, explaining a recommendation or choice I've made that they may realize is only one option of many.*

This icon indicates that the associated note is of special interest to new VFP users, such as MySQL database developers.

Chapter 1
Prepare your development environment

This short chapter gets you up and running in the VFP IDE, and tells you about installation requirements for using VFP in the book's tutorial exercises.

If you have not already done so, you must install Visual FoxPro 9.0 on one of the supported versions of Windows to begin this tutorial.

To follow the final section of the tutorial, you must include the InstallShield Express Visual FoxPro Limited Edition, an optional component, when you install VFP.

> *VFP 9.0 is required for many of the features you'll use in this process; an earlier version will not work.*

> *If you are already a VFP 9.0 user, be aware that use of the default Report Output Application, Report Builder Application, and Report Preview Application is assumed. If you have substituted other versions of the default REPORT*.APP files, some of the dialogs you see may be different and some of the customization features in the final portions of this tutorial may not apply.*

If you are new to MySQL and want to use it for this tutorial, you need to install MySQL too, of course. You can find full documentation, including the various language editions, here http://dev.mysql.com/doc/. For example, the German language edition index page for the on-line version is http://dev.mysql.com/doc/mysql/de/index.html.

> *During the time I wrote this book, MySQL version 5.0 was beta-tested and released. Although there are performance benefits to the new version, there are no changes relevant to the access techniques presented here. Everything described in this book should be relevant to any version of MySQL, just as they would be relevant to Oracle, SQL Server, or other data sources.*

You should also install a MySQL ODBC driver on your computer. You do not need to create any DSNs in Windows' DataSource (ODBC) Administrator tool.

> *The instructions in this document have been tested with the MyODBC driver version 3.51.9. They should work with MyODBC drivers versions 3.51.11 or higher, including 4.x driver releases. However, they do not rely on any 4.x driver features, such as multi-statement queries. Do not use MyODBC driver version 3.51.10, which has critical failures in VFP.*

Ensure that the World database is available from your chosen database server, and you're ready to access it in VFP.

Chapter 2
Bring your data into Visual FoxPro

You're ready to get to work. This chapter shows you how to access and explore your data interactively in the VFP IDE.

When you start up VFP 9.0 for the first time, you may see a helper application such as the Task Pane Manager, as shown on the left in Figure 1.

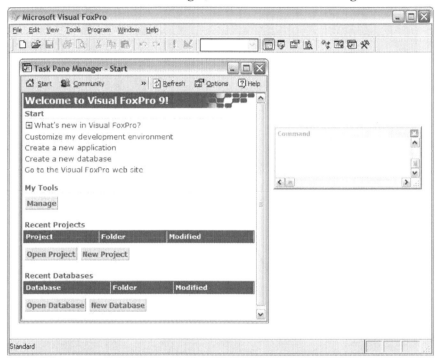

Figure 1. Starting up Visual FoxPro 9.0.

You may want to take time learning to customize your development environment and explore various ways the Task Pane Manager can help you organize your work in VFP later. For now, close the Task Pane window or any other Wizard-like interface that appears, and focus your attention on the Command Window, at the right in Figure 1. You will type a few simple commands in the Command Window to experiment with your MySQL data.

After closing the Task Pane Manager, size the Command Window so you have plenty of room. Type the command below into the Command Window, substituting your server name for **localhost** and using the correct version of the ODBC driver for your system (whether for SQL Server or MySQL).

Press Enter after the command, as if you were executing a command at the DOS command prompt.

Although it may wrap in the example below, be sure to type it all on one line before pressing Enter:

```
myString = "DRIVER=MySQL ODBC 3.51
Driver;SERVER=localhost;DATABASE=world;"
```

Although nothing appears to have happened, this command created a variable and assigned it a value.

You can add to the value of the string stored in the variable as follows; substitute your user name and password for **XX** and **YY** as required. As before, this should be typed on only one line although it may wrap as you see it in this text (remember to press Enter only at the *end* of this command):

```
myString = myString +
"USER=XX;PASSWORD=YY;OPTIONS=3;"
```

If you are using SQL Server, omit the **OPTIONS=3;** section of this string.

You now have a complete connection string which you can use to give VFP a connection to your MySQL or SQL Server World database.

> *If you are familiar with MyODBC driver settings, you may be wondering why I specified the OPTIONS flags in my connection string. This particular combination of binary option flags (1 + 2) is recommended for Visual Basic use and it works well with VFP.*
>
> *Refer to http://dev.mysql.com/doc/mysql/en/connection-parameters.html for the full set of option flags available. For reporting purposes you may also want to add 2097152 or other option flags that improve performance.*
>
> *The driver allows you to specify the flags as an expression, allowing you to list all the values and improving clarity. For example:*

```
myString = myString+"OPTIONS=1 + 2+ 2097152;"
```

You can use this connection string in combination with the VFP SQLSTRINGCONNECT function, as follows:

```
? SQLSTRINGCONNECT(myString)
```

When you execute this command, you see a number echoed to the main VFP window (often called "Screen"), as shown in Figure 2. The "**?**" you used in the command was a print instruction, causing the return value of the function to be sent to Screen.

The return value you see in Screen is a connection handle, which you can use to access the database to which you connected until you close the connection.

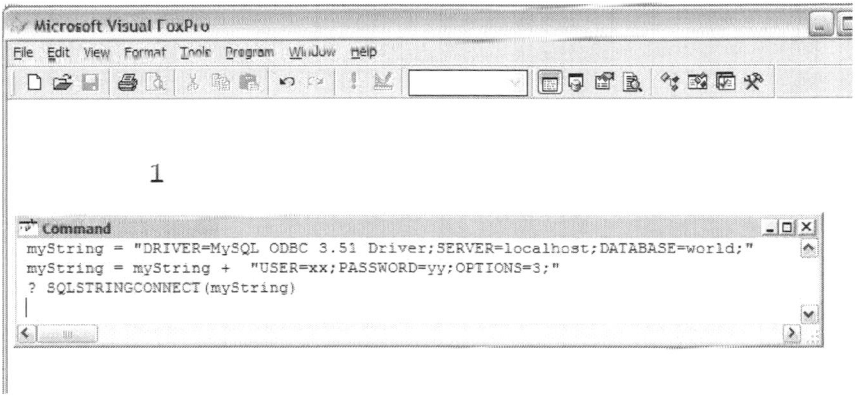

Figure 2. Connecting to MySQL.

If you are familiar with VFP, you know there are many ways besides the SQLSTRINGCONNECT function to set up connections to external data. You may also be surprised that this tutorial uses cursoradapters rather than cursors in many of its instructions.

I'm using the method shown here because it provides a very flexible way to design connections at runtime in an unknown environment. It does not assume setup on the client, other than availability of the ODBC driver, and does not assume that the developer uses VFP DBC containers to manage connections, etc. It also requires a minimum of code.

You can use any method you prefer, but you will discover that this technique is particularly good for generic reporting applications even if you are comfortable writing VFP code.

You're now ready to try out the data connection. Substitute the number you saw on the screen for 1 in the first command below, if VFP reported a different connection handle earlier (don't forget to press Enter after each of the two commands below):

```
SQLEXEC(1,"SELECT * FROM COUNTRY ORDER BY
Continent, Region ")
```

```
SET
```

When you issue the SQLEXEC command above, if you have a slow connection to a remote machine, you may see a small window in the upper right corner of Screen as the query executes. You may not see anything happening, unless you notice the VFP status bar, at the bottom of Screen, as shown in Figure 3 below.

When the second command, SET, executes, VFP's Data Session (or "View") window appears in Screen. The Data Session Window is a handy way to explore data interactively in VFP. Right now, it shows you a cursor holding the data that VFP fetched from MySQL, with the alias Sqlresult.

A cursor in VFP holds the cached result of your query. The VFP cursor's alias provides a way to reference that result when you manipulate the data in additional code, just as the variable myString you used earlier gives you a way to reference the data you stored in the variable. Aliases, column names, and variables in VFP follow the same naming rules as labels and variables in PHP, except that they are not case-sensitive.

> *If you have used ADO with MySQL in a client such as Visual Basic, the cursors I recommend for reporting in VFP are similar to ADO's adOpenStatic type.*
>
> *For the record, you can use ADO with VFP as well as ODBC, and you can use different types of cursors with VFP, but the additional overhead does not provide any advantages for reporting purposes.*

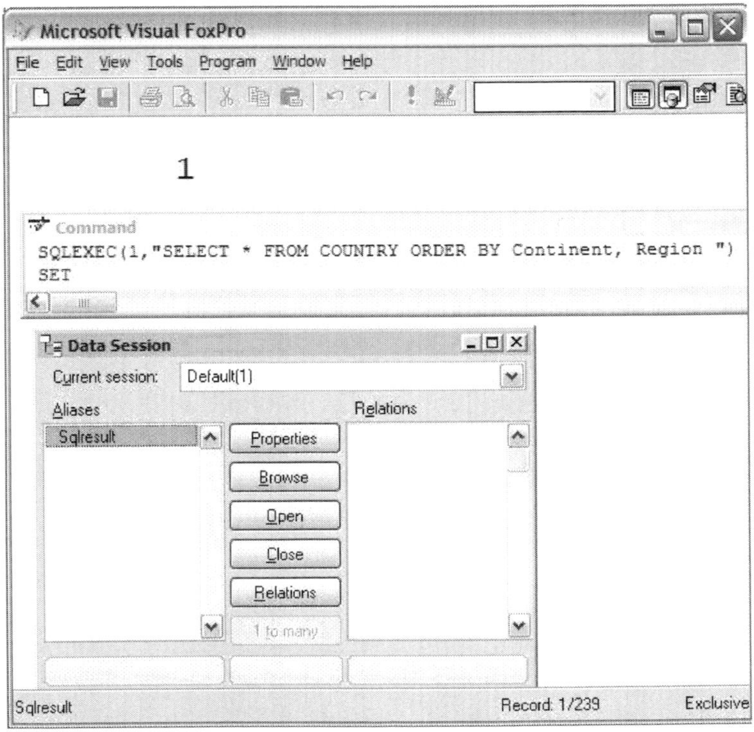

Figure 3. Fetching MySQL Data interactively in VFP's IDE.

If you press the Browse button in the Data Session Window, or double-click on the Sqlresult alias, you can scroll through your data in the Sqlresult cursor, as shown in Figure 4. The Browse window that appears is similar to the scrolling windows you see in the MySQL Query Browser tool (http://www.mysql.com/products/query-browser/).

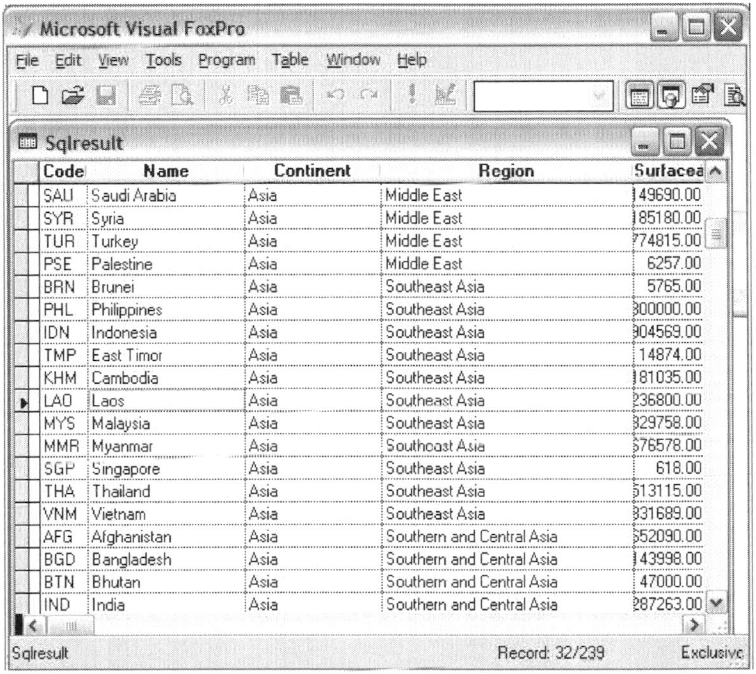

Code	Name	Continent	Region	Surfacea
SAU	Saudi Arabia	Asia	Middle East	49690.00
SYR	Syria	Asia	Middle East	85180.00
TUR	Turkey	Asia	Middle East	74815.00
PSE	Palestine	Asia	Middle East	6257.00
BRN	Brunei	Asia	Southeast Asia	5765.00
PHL	Philippines	Asia	Southeast Asia	00000.00
IDN	Indonesia	Asia	Southeast Asia	04569.00
TMP	East Timor	Asia	Southeast Asia	14874.00
KHM	Cambodia	Asia	Southeast Asia	81035.00
LAO	Laos	Asia	Southeast Asia	36800.00
MYS	Malaysia	Asia	Southeast Asia	29758.00
MMR	Myanmar	Asia	Southeast Asia	76578.00
SGP	Singapore	Asia	Southeast Asia	618.00
THA	Thailand	Asia	Southeast Asia	13115.00
VNM	Vietnam	Asia	Southeast Asia	31689.00
AFG	Afghanistan	Asia	Southern and Central Asia	52090.00
BGD	Bangladesh	Asia	Southern and Central Asia	43998.00
BTN	Bhutan	Asia	Southern and Central Asia	47000.00
IND	India	Asia	Southern and Central Asia	87263.00

Figure 4. Exploring your data in a Browse.

As you can see in the Browse window, the data you received from the SQLEXEC command, using standard SQL syntax, gives you exactly the results you would expect if you used this SQL in any other programming environment. For example, you can see that the data is in the order you specified in the SQL ORDER BY clause.

You can continue to use the data connection for other SQL commands you wish to apply to the same MySQL server instance. When you're finished with the connection, dispose of it with the SQLDISCONNECT(<handle>) command:

```
SQLDISCONNECT(1)
```

Although you have closed the data connection to MySQL, the cursor of MySQL data you fetched into VFP still remains, as you can see in the Data Session Window. You can dispose of the cursor by using the Close button in the Data Session Window, or issue the following command to tell VFP you don't need it any more. In the command, you specify the VFP cursor to close by using its alias:

USE IN sqlresult

And that's it! That's all the FoxPro syntax you have to learn to access external data.

As you've seen, most of the "important work" is done in the SQL syntax you already know and love. You can design your queries in the tool of your choice, such as the MySQL Query Browser, and import them into VFP as text statements, for immediate use.

Now you can start creating report results from your data.

Chapter 3
Create reports

In this section, you'll use exactly the same syntax to access data that you used earlier, this time within a FoxPro report. You will learn some simple techniques for report design.

Before you start creating reports, you may want to navigate Visual FoxPro's current working directory to a location appropriate to saving the files you will create in this tutorial. You can use the DOS commands MD and CD in the Command Window. For example:

```
MD C:\MyReports

CD C:\MyReports
```

As usual, press Enter after each command. Enclose the fully-pathed directory name in quotation marks (either single or double) if the path name contains spaces.

3.1 Adjust the VFP IDE

Before beginning, make one change in the Visual FoxPro environment by using the command **SET REPORTBEHAVIOR 90** in the Command Window.

This instruction sets VFP 9 to use the newer of its two report-rendering engines. Although both engines will work well for most of the work you'll do in VFP reporting, the newer version requires slightly more space to render text. By specifying this style before designing a report, you ensure that the text layout controls you create are sized with enough space for use with either rendering engine.

If you wish to make this setting permanent, go to the **Tools** *menu and choose* **Options...** *from the menu list. In the* **Options** *dialog's* **Reports** *panel, shown in Figure 5, set the* **Report Engine** *behavior dropdown to 90 (Object-Assisted), and click the* **Set As Default** *button.*

You can also set an option, **Century** *(1998 vs 98), in this dialog's* **Regional** *panel, to ensure that any date expressions are sized with plenty of room. The command to set this in the Command Window is* **SET CENTURY ON**.

When you review the **Regional** *panel, you may want to ensure that Visual Fox-Pro defaults for date expressions and other locale-sensitive output are formatted appropriately for your language and culture. Although these items can be re-set within* *reports, it is a good idea to verify their default settings in this dialog so you don't have to adjust them individually for each expression.*

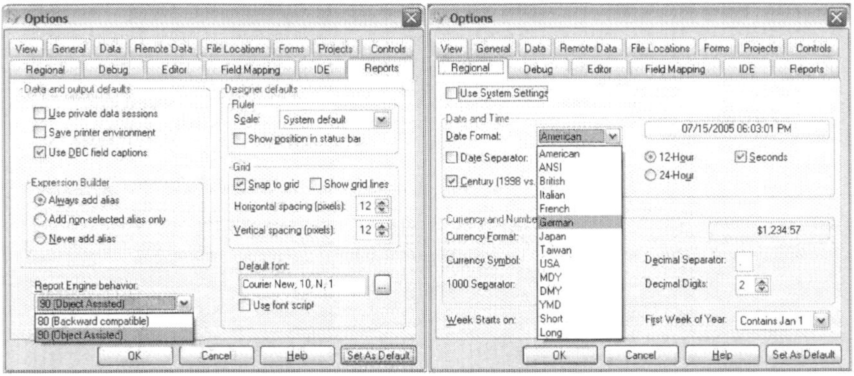

Figure 5. VFP's Tools Options dialog has a panel to set Report-specific items such as Report Engine behavior, and a separate panel with Regional settings that are also significant to reports.

3.2 Open the VFP Report Designer

To start designing the report, open the VFP Report Designer. You can do this by selecting **New...** on the **File** menu, and then selecting **Report** as your file type from the dialog. If you would like to use the Command Window, you can type **CREATE REPORT**.

When the Report Designer window opens, it looks something like Figure 6 below. You notice three "bands", or report design areas, separated by "band separator bars": a page header, a page footer, and a detail band. The report content you place in the detail band repeats once for every record in your cursor, and the report content in the page header and footer repeats once for every page.

3.3 Add data instructions to the report

Right-click any where on the Report Designer area except the band separator bars, and choose the **Data Environment...** option you see in its context menu.

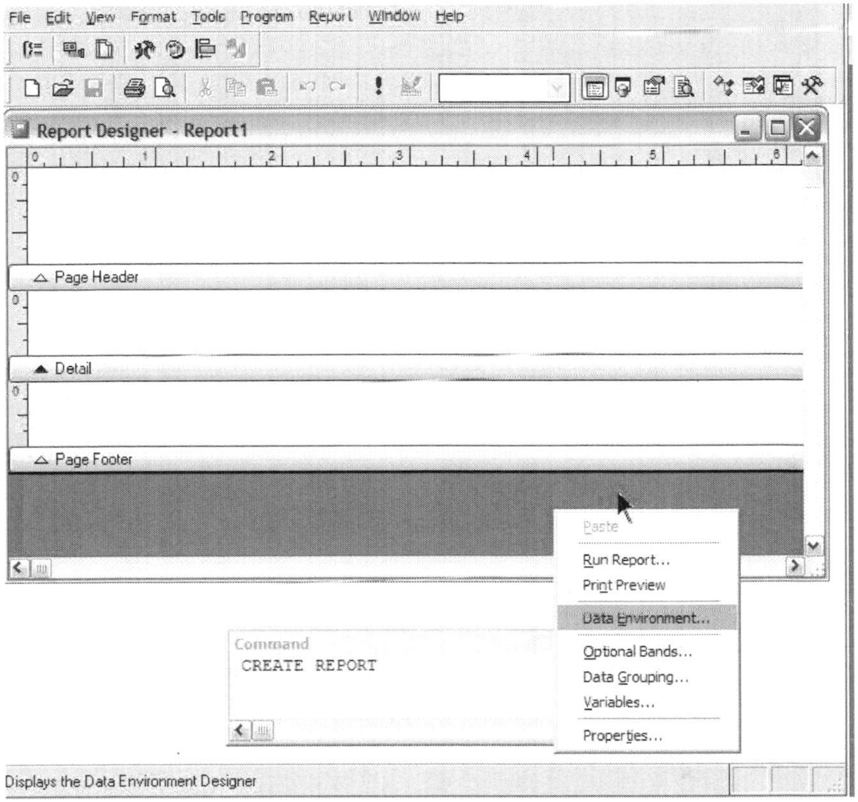

Figure 6. Begin a report design session by accessing the report's Data Environment from the Report Designer window.

After you choose this option, a new window, the Data Environment Designer, opens. It shows you another shaded design area, initially blank. When you right-click in the Data Environment Designer you get another context menu.

The first item, **Add...**, is used to add local Xbase tables (DBFs) to the Data Environment. Choose the second option on the context menu to Add CursorAdapter, as indicated in Figure 7.

> *A cursoradapter object in Visual FoxPro provides a way to handle cursors representing data that has been fetched into local FoxPro cursors, usually from external data sources. When the external data is represented as cursoradapter objects, it can be more easily manipulated as objects in VFP IDE design windows and in VFP application code.*

A "placeholder" cursoradapter appears in the Data Environment Designer window. Your next task is to give this cursoradapter object some information about the data you plan to use in the report, including the same data connection information you used in the Command Window earlier.

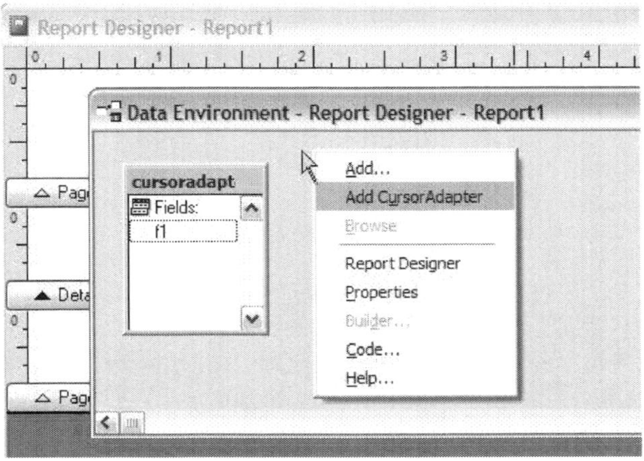

Figure 7. Get ready to add a cursoradapter to your report's Data Environment.

Right-click again on the Data Environment Designer surface, and choose **Properties** from the context menu. You can now see the Properties Window, a tabbed palette that allows you to set the properties of the general Data Environment for your report and for each data object within the Data Environment. By selecting different objects in the Data Environment Designer with your mouse, or by using the dropdown at the top of the Properties Window, you can select which object you wish to edit. To examine general settings for the **Data Environment**, select it from the dropdown, as shown in Figure 8.

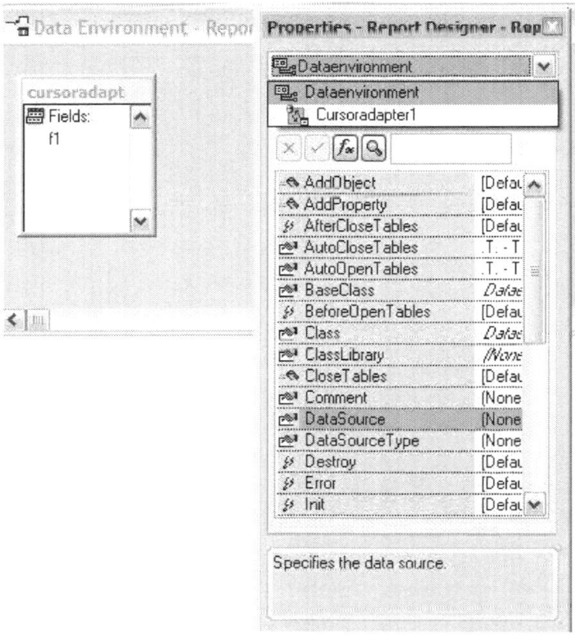

Figure 8. Edit the Data Environment in the Properties Window.

In the Properties Window, you see a list of all the attributes (on the left, in gray in Figure 8) for the currently-selected object, and the attributes' current values (on the right, in white). Above these lists, and below the object drop-down, you also see a row of small buttons and an input box.

As you highlight different attributes in the Properties Window list, these buttons and the input box change dynamically. For example, In Figure 8, they are enabled, indicating that you can type a DataSource value directly into the input box or press the "Zoom" button (with a magnifying glass icon) to edit this value with more space. If you highlight the DataSourceType value, next in the list, the button disables and the input box changes to a dropdown. This change indicates that DataSourceType is an enumerated type. You cycle through the available values by double-clicking directly in the value region for this attribute (which currently reads (None)) or by choosing a value from the dropdown.

> *You may not be able to see exactly what shows in Figure 8 when you initially invoke the Properties Window. For example, you may not be able to see that the **DataSourceType** attribute follows **DataSource**; both attribute names may be truncated in the list.*

Give yourself more space by resizing the Properties Window; click-drag its bottom right corner. Resize the columns in the attribute list by click-dragging the on the area separating the attribute and value columns. The window does not display a separator bar, but your mouse cursor changes when you're in the right region.

Select the **cursoradapter1** object from the object dropdown. Specify the values of five cursoradapter attributes:

1. Change the Alias to match the data you're using in the report. This step is optional but it helps to use aliases that really tell you what data you're using in the report, just as you use descriptive variable names and labels in PHP. In Figure 9, I've used the alias **Country**, to match the name of the underlying MySQL table.

2. Add a SelectCmd value, using standard SQL syntax, similar to what you used earlier. It is easiest to do this by pressing the "Zoom" button (with the magnifying glass icon) to reach You can use **SELECT** * as you did before but, for production use in reporting, you want to specify the fields you intend to use in the report rather than requesting all columns. Here is the SELECT statement I've used in this example:

   select Continent, GNP, GNPOld, GovernmentForm, HeadOfState, IndepYear, LifeExpectancy, LocalName, Name, Population, Region from country order by Continent, Region

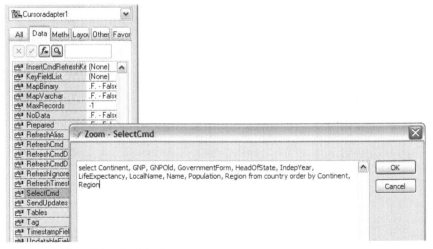

Figure 9. Adding a SelectCmd for the report.

The SELECT statement you have typed executes when you run this report, but the Report Designer does not know anything about what your data should look like at this point. You give the Designer a little extra help by changing the **CursorSchema** attribute. By default, it reads "**f1 c(10)**", which does not describe your data at all. Change the value of this attribute to match your SELECT statement, using the following expression:

```
CONTINENT    C(13),    GNP    B(2),    GNPOLD    B(2),
GOVERNMENTFORM C(44),  HEADOFSTATE C(33), INDEPYEAR
I,   LIFEEXPECTANCY   B(2),   LOCALNAME   C(44),   NAME
C(44), POPULATION I, REGION C(25)
```

Notice that this list of columns is roughly equivalent to how you would specify the same fields in a CREATE TABLE statement in SQL, although it specifies some of the types slightly differently than MySQL and the ANSI SQL standard. For example, you can use C(<length>) for a character-type field instead of CHAR(<length>). Both *C(<length>) and CHAR(<length>) work in VFP*.

> *In many cases, you can use the MySQL command* **SHOW CREATE TABLE <name>** *to get exactly what you need for the CursorSchema contents. Simply remove the extra clauses on each column (such as AUTOINCREMENT, NOT NULL, or default <value>) and the delimiters around column names. In SQL Server or other databases, you find similar tools for scripting or generating CREATE TABLE statements.*

> *The VFP help file has a topic titled* **CREATE CURSOR - SQL Command** *with a complete list of the available types and the keywords you can use to specify them, some of which have several alternatives.*

> *Where your MySQL data type does not have a direct analog, such as MEDIUMINT, you can find an appropriate substitute in this table. For MEDIUMINT, the appropriate substitute would be Integer, which you describe using the keyword I, INT, or INTEGER.*

1. Change the DataSourceType value to ODBC, using the drop-down or by cycling through the types by double-clicking the value area for this attribute.

2. Change the **DataSource** to an expression representing the result of the same **SQLStringConnect** command you used in the Command Window. As shown in Figure 10, I recommend using the "Zoom" window for this value as you did for the **SelectCmd** and **CursorSchema**. You type the full SQLSTRINGCONNECT command you used in the Command Window earlier, substituting a bracket-delimited string with the full connection string for the variable you used, and adding an "=" (equal) sign at the beginning of your expression. The equal sign tells the

Data Environment that you want the result of this expression, the connection handle, to be stored as the value of the DataSource attribute, not the expression itself. Although it may wrap below, type the full string without pressing the "Enter" key: **=SQLSTRINGCONNECT([DRIVER=MySQL ODBC 3.51 Driver;SERVER=localhost;DATABASE=world;USER=XX ;PASSWORD=YY;OPTIONS=3;])**

Don't forget to replace the driver version, server, user and password values you see above as appropriate for your database.

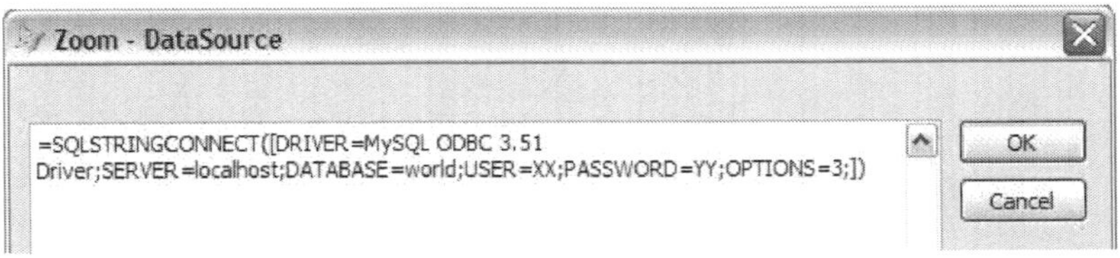

Figure 10. Specify a connection handle for the report in the Data Environment DataSource attribute.

Although you store the server, user and password values directly in the FRX file for this exercise, you do not have to do so for production use. I will show you other ways to provide these values at runtime, later in this tutorial.

You have now specified enough information about the data to begin designing your report. If you right-click on the object dropdown and choose to "collapse" the attribute list down to only the values you have edited, you should see something like Figure 11.

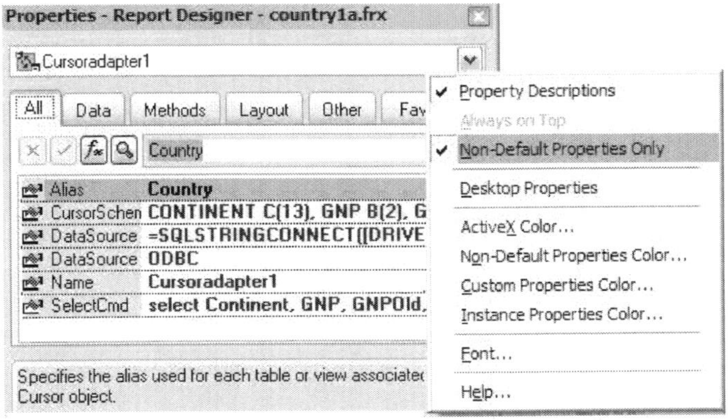

Figure 11. Your edited properties for the cursoradapter.

You can "collapse" the Properties Window's attribute list in this way any time you want to check the work you've done. You also notice that non-default values in the full list are bolded and colored to draw your attention to them.

Returning your attention to the Data Environment Designer, you see that the representation of the cursor now matches your data (see Figure 12).

Place your mouse cursor on the title bar (with the word "**Country**") of your cursoradapter object in the Data Environment window, to select the full cursoradapter contents. Drag it directly to the area above the band separator marked **Detail Band** in the Report Designer.

The cursoradapter object does not change or move, but you see the mouse cursor change to a representation of several "stacked" rectangles. There is a brief pause and the Detail Band area changes size to make room for all the fields you specified in the CursorSchema attribute.

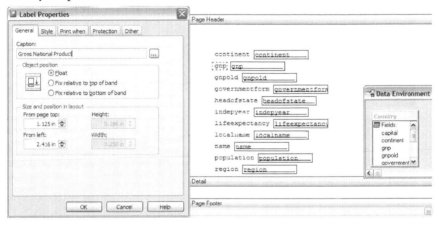

Figure 12. Drag and drop your data into the report layout, and make simple adjustments to the contents.

The Detail Band now shows data content, with each cursor column having a label followed by a rectangular box showing the expression the Report Engine uses to display the data at runtime.

The paired labels and expressions match your specified column names, by default. You can change the labels to more appropriate description of the columns; for example "**Gross National Product**" instead of "**GNP**". Double-click on a label and its Properties dialog appears, as shown in Figure 12.

You may need to move the label in the Report layout after doing this, to make enough room for the new, longer label. You can move the label in several ways:

- Use the **Size and position in layout** settings in the Label Properties dialog.

- Select it with the mouse and drag it to the new position.

- Use the Tab key to cycle through the controls in the layout until the label shows selection handles at its four corners. Then "nudge" the label into position with the arrow keys.

3.4 Save and run the report

Your report is now ready to run.

Use the **File** menu's **Save As** option to save the report with a suitable name. I have used **Country1a** in your source code. (All the reports are saved to the "develop\reports" directory of your sample files.)

> *The **FRX** file extension is included by default. It is not required, but I recommend you use it consistently. You also see a second file, with an **FRT** extension. A Visual FoxPro report definition file is actually a VFP table, and it requires two files to store long text and blob fields, such as the connection string, in associated memofields.*

Use the **File** menu's **Print Preview** option to view the results. You see a brief progress bar, and then a display similar to Figure 13. (If you did not **SET REPORTBEHAVIOR 90** earlier, the progress bar does not appear and the display looks slightly different.) As you page through the contents, or use the preview toolbar to move through the report pages, notice that you have one instance of each record in the Country table. For each instance, you see the column labels repeated and the column expression evaluated, providing the data contents.

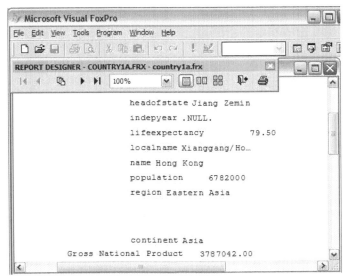

Figure 13. Previewing a report from the Report Designer.

You have accomplished all the required steps to create and run VFP reports using your data. You're ready to design more sophisticated layouts and present more complex data.

To start, make a few changes in the Data Environment that, while not required for this report, are helpful for more complex data. As you'll see in this tutorial, VFP gives you several ways to share data settings between reports, so it is a good idea to use settings consistently.

Use the Exit button (with the picture of a door) on the preview toolbar, or press the Esc key, to return to the Report Designer. Use the **File** menu's **Save As...** option to save the report to a new name (I've used **Country1b** in the samples). You adjust the data settings in this copy of the report.

> *You can also save the report, or any other file you edit in VFP of any type, by pressing* **Ctrl-S**. *You can save and close any file you're editing by pressing* **Ctrl-W**.

3.5 Improve your Data Environment settings

Use the context menu to invoke the Data Environment Designer, as you did earlier, and invoke the Properties Window if you do not see it already. If you set the attributes list in the Properties Window to show Non-Default Properties Only earlier, return the display to the full list of attributes now.

First, adjust the values of cursoradapter attributes:

1. Change the value of the **UseDeDataSource** attribute, an enumerated type, to **.T. (True)**. This setting tells the report that the default connection you set up for the Data Environment should be used for this cursoradapter object.

   > *I recommend you use this setting for most reporting work; it is best to share one connection.*

   > *Make an exception, and use multiple connections, if you are using multiple data sources in your report. In this case, you need one connection per data source. For example, you could join data between your MySQL database and an Oracle database in the report. In this case, you might have a "main" data connection for MySQL and then specify a* **DataSource** *and a* **DataSourceType** *for each Oracle-based cursoradapter, which does not share the "main" data connection for the report.*

   > *You'll discover that, once each source is cached in a Visual FoxPro cursor, you can use standard SQL syntax on the cursors to manipulate the data as if it all came from a single data source. This can be extremely efficient and convenient.*

2. Scroll to the **DataSource** attribute in the attribute list. Its value should be highlighted in the input box at the top of the Properties Window, or in the "Zoom" window if you invoke it. Press Ctrl-A to ensure that the entire string is selected, and then Ctrl-C to copy this string. You move the connection information to the Data Environment in your next step. Now you can remove this information from the cursoradapter instructions. You can remove the value manually (press backspace) or by right-clicking on the attribute line and selecting **Reset to Default** from the context menu.

3. Remove the **DataSourceType** information as well. This step is not required – a type of ODBC does no harm if there is no source listed – but removing this value reminds you that this cursoradapter is sharing a connection.

Figure 14 shows you default information restored for **DataSource** and the context menu active for **DataSourceType**, ready to **Reset to Default**.

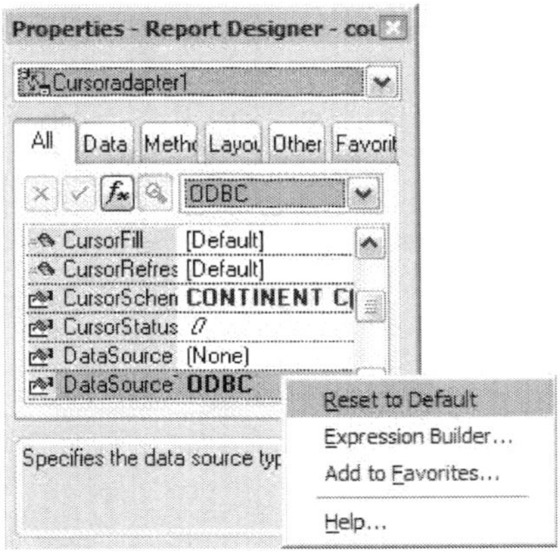

Figure 14. Resetting values to default in the Properties Window.

Now turn your attention to the Data Environment object's properties by selecting this object in the object drop down. Change the values of three attributes for the Data Environment:

1. Change the **Initially Selected Alias** to the name you gave your cursor. This step is not required for a simple report, but it is a good habit. The attribute is an enumerated type, so you cycle through the alias names for all the objects currently in your Data Environment. In the example, the value you want is **Country**.

2. Change the **DataSource** to an expression representing the result of the same SQLSTRINGCONNECT command you used for the cursoradapter earlier. You should be able to paste it directly into the Zoom window, if you copied it while adjusting the cursoradapter in the last step. Otherwise, type it in from scratch, including the leading "=" sign and quotation marks as before.

3. Change the **DataSourceType** value to ODBC as you did for the cursoradapter earlier.

Save the report and preview it, as you did for the first report. The preview results are the same.

Now that you know how to get your data into VFP reports, how do you get the reports to look the way you want? For help with this perplexing question, turn to the next chapter.

Chapter 4
Customize your report layouts

For your first reports, you dragged a representation of your cursor data into the layout. You can also move individual columns into the layout by dragging and dropping them from the Data Environment, so you can position them more exactly.

In this section, you learn another simple way to get your data into the layout, and then start customizing the layout more completely.

4.1 Quick-start report designs

If you have been following the instructions so far, and have not used SQLDISCONNECT() to remove any connections, you have at least one active connection handle to your MySQL database in the current Visual FoxPro session: the connection you created in the Command Window and additional connections created by the Report Designer when it evaluated your **DataSource** expression in the Properties Window.

For production use, you manage your connections more carefully, as you learn in a later section, but for your design sessions, it's okay to have these extra connections. You can close them explicitly with SQLDISCONNECT(), or they close automatically when you exit Visual FoxPro.

If you have just started a new session of Visual FoxPro, ensure that you have a connection handle available, using the technique you used earlier. Use the connection handle value in a SQLEXEC statement as you did before, but this time add a third parameter to the function, specifying a cursor alias for the command to use instead of the default SQLResult:

SQLEXEC(1,"SELECT * FROM COUNTRY ORDER BY Continent, Region ", "Country")

Using the Data Session Window, or the status bar, verify that you have a cursor open and selected with the alias Country. If it is not currently selected (highlighted in the Data Session Window's list of Aliases or displaying in the status bar), select it in the window list or use the command SELECT Country in the Command Window.

Now choose to create a new report as you did earlier. When the Report Designer window appears, first choose the **Default Font...** option from the Report menu, and designate your base font for this report. Next, choose the **Quick Report...** option from the Report menu. The Quick Report Dialog, shown in Figure 15 below, appears.

> *In the dialog, notice the option to* **Add alias**. *This option, checked by default, affects the way the Quick Report generates expressions for the data in your table columns. Although for a simple report based on one cursor, you do not need to use aliases, it is a good habit to use them. You used the third argument in the last SQLEXEC statement to specify your alias, to ensure that Quick Report would give you the appropriate alias in each expression.*

In the Quick Report dialog, you can click the **Fields...** button to get to a nested Field Picker dialog. Select some fields you used in the earlier reports. In Figure 16, I've used Continent, Region, and Name.

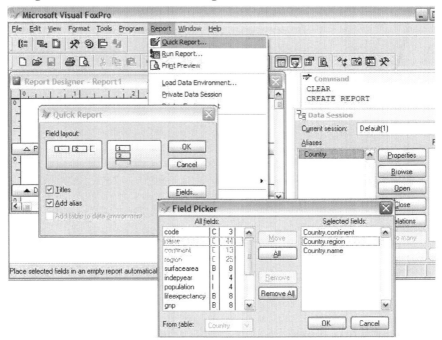

Figure 15. Building a Quick Report.

Having selected your field list, press **OK** in the Field Picker dialog, and then press **OK** again in the Quick Report dialog to generate the report contents. The Report Designer window's contents should resemble Figure 16. The exact contents depend on the default font and fields you chose.

Notice that the columns are laid out across the page, with the labels listed in bold type in the page header band, in contrast to the "form" layout you got earlier when you dragged the cursoradapter object from the Data Environment.

This columnar layout, with the column labels repeated only once per page, is appropriate for many types of reports. The Quick Report dialog gives you the option of either style of layout, by toggling the **Field layout** buttons you see in Figure 15.

Save this report as **Country2**, and preview the report. It appears as shown in Figure 17.

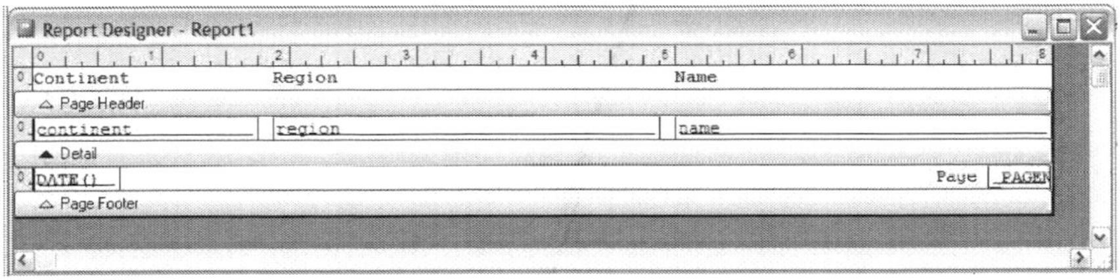

Figures 16 (above) and 17 (below). Quick Report layout and preview results.

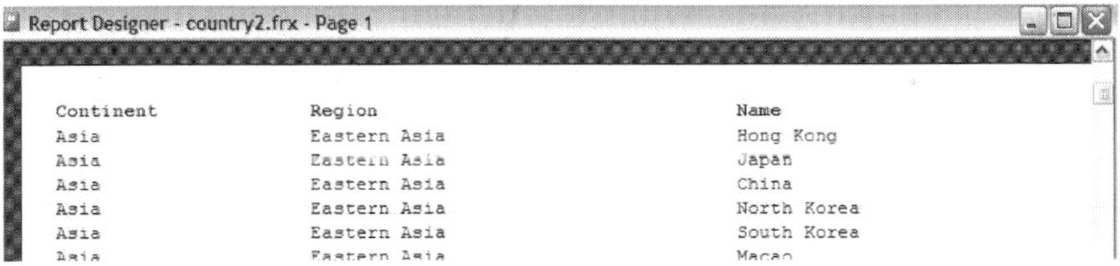

As you can see, VFP finds the necessary data available, because you explicitly issued a SQLEXEC statement in the Command Window. (You created the cursor to make it available to Quick Report.)

How can VFP find the data when you run this report in an application?

In your other reports, you added the necessary instructions to the report's Data Environment. You can do the same thing for this report, but you do not have to recreate the instructions.

4.2 Load the Data Environment from a similar report

This report uses the same cursor alias and the same basic data as your previous reports. You can include the same data environment in this report as before, by choosing the **Load Data Environment...** option from the Report menu. Choose the option to **Copy from another report file** in the Report Properties dialog, and click the **Select...** button. Choose either of the reports you have already designed from the Open dialog, shown in Figure 18.

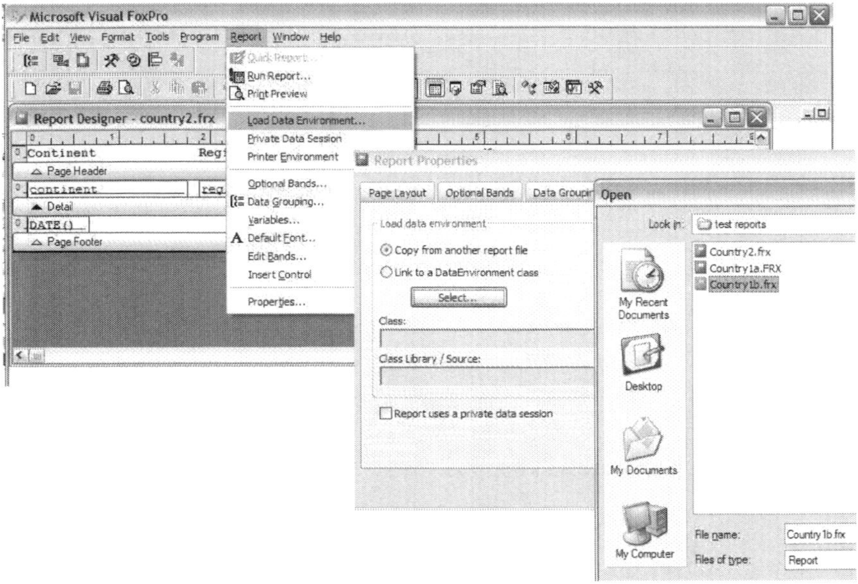

Figure 18. Loading another FRX's Data Environment.

When you press **OK** in the Open dialog you see two dialogs. The first reminds you that you are about to replace the current Data Environment in the current report (it is currently empty), and the second reminds you that you must save your changes in the Report Properties dialog to have these changes take effect. After these two reminders, you are back in the Report Properties dialog, and your chosen report filename shows in the box labeled **Class Library/Source**. Press **OK** again to save your changes in the Report Properties dialog, as you were instructed, and you are returned to the Report Designer.

The new report now contains your Data Environment instructions. Save this report again to finalize its contents.

To verify the availability of the data from the new report, first give yourself a "fresh start" by clearing out all available data and connections in the Visual FoxPro environment. Using the Data Session Window, or the command **CLOSE DATA** in the Command Window, ensure that the Country cursor is no longer open. Close the Report Designer and issue the following command in the Command Window: **SQLDISCONNECT(0)**. The "0" argument to the SQLDISCONNECT function ensures that all open connections are closed.

4.3 Test-run the report and its data-handling

This time, run the report without opening the Report Designer, to make sure the Report Designer doesn't open any connections automatically.

In the Command Window, or in Visual FoxPro programs, you run reports using the command **REPORT FORM <filename>**. This command has many options, including a **PREVIEW** keyword to use when you want to see the report on-screen. In this case, run the report from the Command Window, using the following syntax:

REPORT FORM Country2 PREVIEW

> *You can replace the filename* **Country2** *with a "?" if you wish to use the Open dialog to find it.*

The report previews as expected. As you scroll through the contents of the preview, you notice that the Quick Report mechanism provided a page footer, with a date and page number, as well as column labels in the page header.

It might be nice to format these items a little differently, and to use them on the reports you created earlier.

4.4 Customize your report layout elements

Open **Country2.FRX** in the Report Designer. You can see the date and page number expressions in the page footer band, shown in Figure 16 above. You can double-click on the expressions to reach their Properties dialogs.

The DATE() function you see in the left-side expression is a built-in function in VFP. Similar to CURDATE() in MySQL or GETDATE() in SQL Server, it returns a VFP date type. (When you need a date-time value in VFP, use the function DATETIME().)

You do not have to worry about converting the result of the DATE() function to a string for reports unless you wish to concatenate it with another string within a more complex report expression (as you learn to do in this section). The Report Engine converts the final results of all expressions, regardless of data type, appropriately for output .

You can use the Format tab in the Field properties dialog to re-format the date; for example, choose **Use long date setting**. Stretch the default width of this layout control and try your preview again, to see the result, as shown in Figure 19.

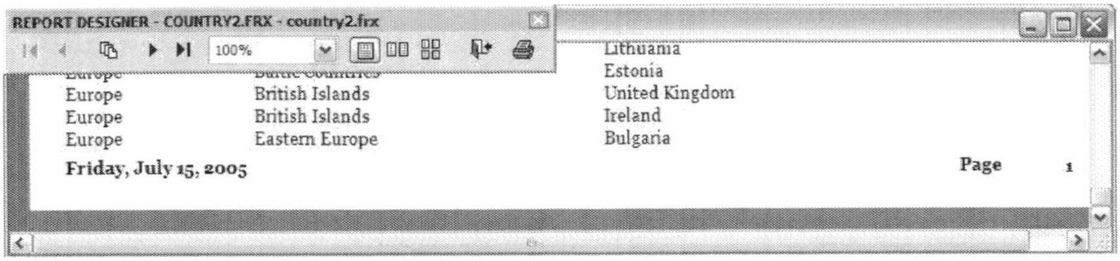

Figure 19. Revising the Quick Report page footer.

The page number expression is a built-in VFP system variable, _PAGENO, which stores an integer value. When you run a report, the Report Engine updates the value of _PAGENO at the beginning of every page, so, when you evaluate _PAGENO in report expressions, its value is correct for each page.

> *You can retain the final value of _PAGENO between reports; use the NORESET keyword on your REPORT FORM command to give the Report Engine this instruction. These capabilities allow you to create page numbering scheme that "continues" throughout a sequence or series of multiple reports.*

As you can see in Figure 19, there may be quite a gap between the label "Page" preceding this number and the page number itself. (Quick Report sizes the page number expression to leave room for very long reports.) To format the expression properly, you may want to concatenate the label and page number and set the spacing yourself.

You can delete the "Page" label from the layout (select it and press the Delete key). Move the _PAGENO expression a bit to the left, and make it larger so there is room for the full concatenated expression. Then access the _PAGENO expression's Field Properties dialog. Type the following expression:

`"PAGE "+TRANSFORM(_PAGENO)`

This expression, shown in Figure 20, instructs the report to use the TRANSFORM(<value>) function on the _PAGENO variable. The result of the TRANSFORM function can be concatenated with the string value `"PAGE "`.

The TRANSFORM function casts any data type to a string, so it is very useful for building complicated report output expressions based on a combination of data columns. It accepts an optional second argument you can use to format the resulting string, something like the FORMAT(<var>,<pattern>) function in VB or printf(<pattern>,<var>) in PHP.

You can type the expression directly into the input box on the General tab of the Field Properties dialog.

Alternatively, you can press the "..." (ellipsis) button, which appears next to the input box in the dialog. This action invokes the nested Expression Builder dialog, which provides some "coaching" on Visual FoxPro functions appropriate to different data types. The Expression Builder dialog appears in Figure 20.

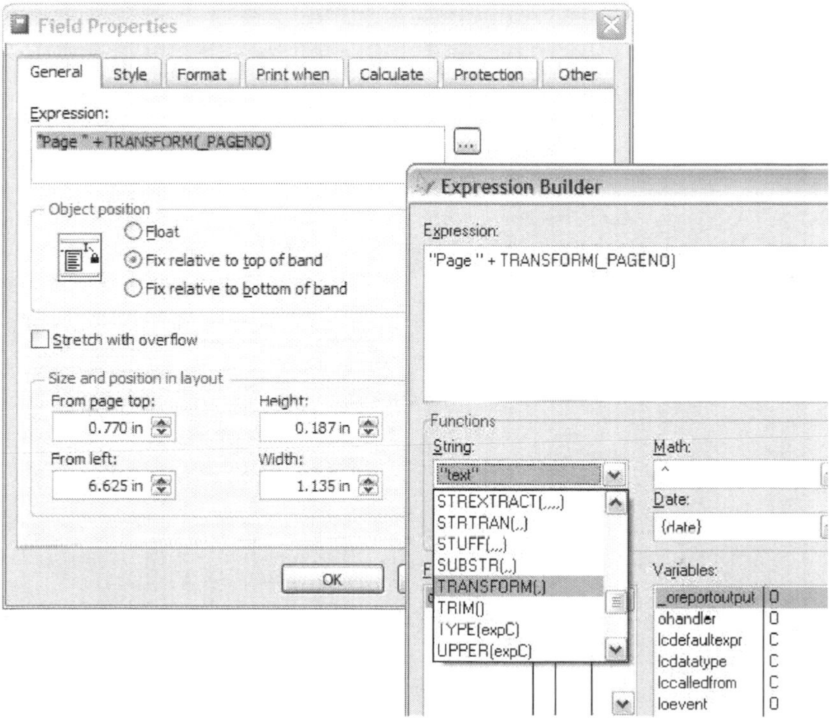

Figure 20. Creating a report expression.

Press the **OK** button in the Field Properties dialog to change the contents of your report layout control. Preview the report again, to see the difference, and save the Country2.FRX report with these changes when you are satisfied with them. (In your samples, I saved it to a new name, Country3.FRX.)

4.5 Use Print When to print expressions selectively

Returning to the Report Designer after preview, you notice that you have Continent and Region values repeating across multiple detail records, because the Country records are ordered by these values in your SELECT statement.

In the next section, you learn to use group bands in reports, but you can change the presentation of your detail band to make it clearer, too.

Access the Field Properties dialog for the Continent expression, and click the **Print When** tab. As shown in Figure 21, you can select an option to omit printing of repeated values of an expression. When you use it, another checkbox is enabled, which allows to you selectively print the repeated value if it occurs on a new page. I checked this option for the sample report.

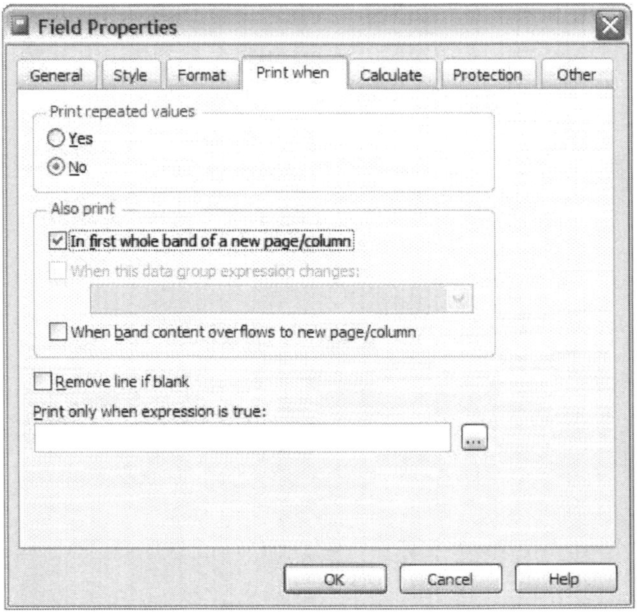

Figure 21. Using Print When for a Field expression in the report.

The **Print When** *dialog tab contains a number of other useful options, not applicable to this report.*

You see a check box to re-print a repeated value when band content overflows. On the **General** *tab of the Field Properties dialog, you can set expressions that evaluate to lengthy strings to wrap and stretch, pushing additional content downward, rather than being cut off at one line. When you use this option, your detail band may span report pages or columns (bands do not have to have a fixed height). In this case, you may want to re-print the repeated values.*

The option to **Remove line if blank** *is useful in cases where you want to close up empty space in an entire line when some items are dynamically suppressed. In this report, this will never happen, because the* **Country.NAME** *value prints on every detail line.*

You also notice an additional option in the dialog, still disabled, to re-print a re-peated value when a data group changes. This option enables when you add groups to the report.

*A final option in this dialog, **Print only when expression is true** allows dy-namic control over output based on any Visual FoxPro expression evaluating to a logical (Boolean) result. You use this option later in the tutorial.*

I selected **Print When** options for both Continent and Region, and saved **Country3.FRX** again. You can see the resulting preview in Figure 22.

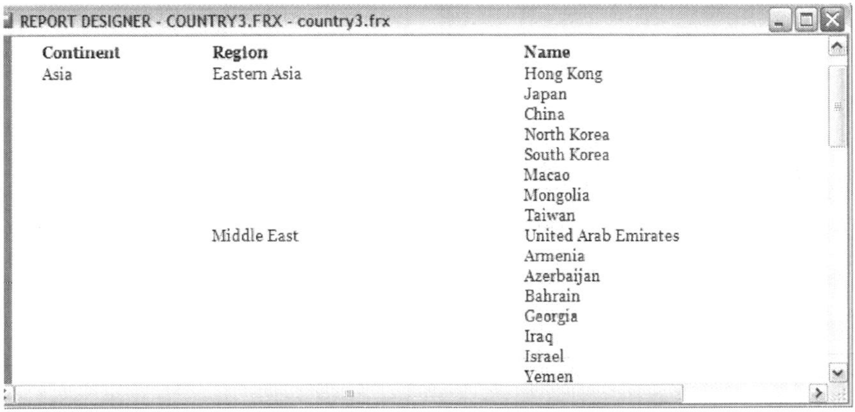

Figure 22. Results of Print When with repeating data elements.

4.6 Repeat, and refine, your layout customizations

Returning to the Report Designer again, you decide you want the same page footer in another report. First, select both layout controls in the page footer. When they are both selected, press Ctrl-C to copy them, or use the equivalent **Copy** choices in the context and **Edit** menus.

> *You can drag a selection marquee around multiple layout controls in the Report Designer, or shift-click to multiple-select controls in the layout as you can in most Windows applications. The Report Designer also has a special shortcut for selecting all the controls in a single band: shift-double-click on the band separator bar (in this case, the page footer).*

You can close this report now, if you want to – but you don't have to. Open another Report Designer window with the report in which you want to use this page footer (**Country1a.FRX** or **Country1b.FRX**).

Paste the layout controls you copied, which were in the page footer in the first report, into the second report layout; they remain selected. Make room in the page footer band by dragging the page footer band separator bar downward and move the new layout controls into this band – or place them in the page header, if you prefer. Use the **Font...** option on the **Format** menu to re-set their font properties as appropriate for this report, if you wish. In your samples, I saved the results to a new report, **Country1c.FRX**.

Experiment with expressions in reports. For example, in **Country1c.FRX**, I decided to change the **"GNPold"** expression to show the difference between the current and old GNP values, and I changed the label to match.

You can see these changes in Figure 23. As you'd expect, the difference between the two GNP values is expressed as a subtraction: **COUNTRY.gnp - COUNTRY.gnpold.**

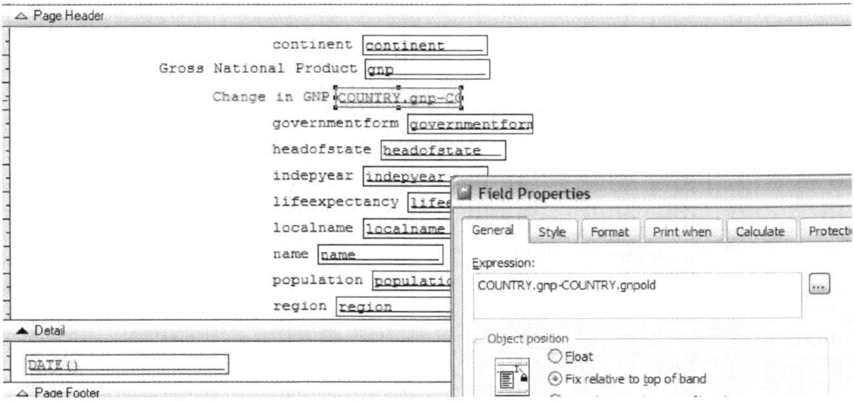

Figure 23. More report layout editing.

> *Remember that, in Visual FoxPro, such expressions, as well as column and table names and keywords in VFP commands, are not case-sensitive.*

4.7 Decide when to use Visual FoxPro expressions

When, and why, should you use Visual FoxPro expressions to format your data?

In many reports you won't need to write any Visual FoxPro expressions, even simple and intuitive ones like the one used here, and you won't have to re-format any expressions. You can do the equivalent work in MySQL as part of your SELECT statement. In this example, simply express the difference of the two values as a column in your cursor.

However, it is often convenient to have the ability to write report expressions, especially when you need to use a column more than once in a report. Calculating an extra column in the report, instead of in the SELECT, means you don't have to send extra data over the network connection. This approach also allows more efficient re-use of generic SQL SELECT expressions for multiple reports.

The more complex your dataset, the more you will appreciate the ability to mix ad-hoc reporting expressions with calculated columns that require work on the server. In the next chapter, you continue your discovery process, investigating the broad and deep VFP options for representing complex data table and record relationships.

Chapter 5
Communicate complex data

We have only skimmed the surface of what you can do, both for calculations on expressions and for formatting your results.

VFP provides a huge number of built-in functions for evaluating, calculating and displaying expressions of all types. The Report Designer surface gives you extensive abilities to size, move, and format controls of the various supported layout control types: labels, expressions, lines, shapes, and pictures. The Properties dialog, which displays tabs specific to each control type, exposes these abilities.

You'll continue to see these options in use, throughout this tutorial. However, a full discussion of these language and design capabilities is beyond our scope. (The Visual FoxPro help file contains full details.)

Now that you have the basics, this section concentrates on report design changes of types that are innately tied to your source data.

5.1 Show data groups

You've seen that Print When expressions can provide visual clues in a report, to organize repeating data into groups. Not every report layout, however, can use this method to provide data grouping.

For example, the report you have been working on the last section (see Figure 23) is organized in a form-based, rather than columnar, layout. If you used Print When expressions to suppress repeated Continent and Region names, it would be difficult to see these groupings in the report results. Instead, you can create group bands, and move the expressions representing the repeating data into these bands.

Group bands "embrace" the detail band with a header and footer. They can be set to start a new page, and to re-start page numbering in a report, if you want. The layout controls in group bands can be formatted completely differently from the detail band.

You can add multiple levels of grouping, similar to the way you concatenate different expressions in the ORDER BY clause for the report data. You set up the group levels in the same order you would place the expressions in the ORDER BY clause, with the outermost group level representing the leftmost expression in the ORDER BY clause.

To begin adding groups to the report in the last section, use the **Data Grouping...** option on the Report menu. (I saved the report to a new name, Country1d.frx, in your samples, first.) Press the **Add** button in the Data Grouping tab of the Report Properties dialog, and the Expression Builder dialog appears. Type the expression that corresponds to your outermost group; in this report, it is **Country.Continent**.

After you press **OK** in the Expression Builder, your group expression appears in the listbox, and you can choose to **Add** another group expression; in this case, **Country.Region**. Refer to Figure 24 to see how the dialogs appear at this point.

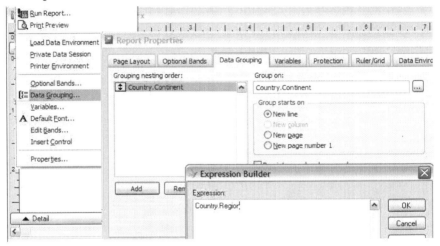

Figure 24. Adding Data Groups to a report from the Report Properties dialog.

When you have saved your changes in the Report Properties dialog and return to the Report Designer layout, it appears with two band pairs: headers and footers for your two group expressions. Drag the group header band separator bars downward, to make room for report layout controls in the header bands. The layout window should resemble Figure 25.

> *If, when you return to the report layout, you find that you have specified the group levels in the wrong order, or need to make any other adjustment to the groups, you can double-click on a group header band separator bar. This action accesses the Group Header Band Properties dialog, also shown in Figure 25. The Group Header Band Properties dialog has a **Data Grouping** tab on which you can rearrange the group levels and perform the related functions available from the Report Properties dialog.*

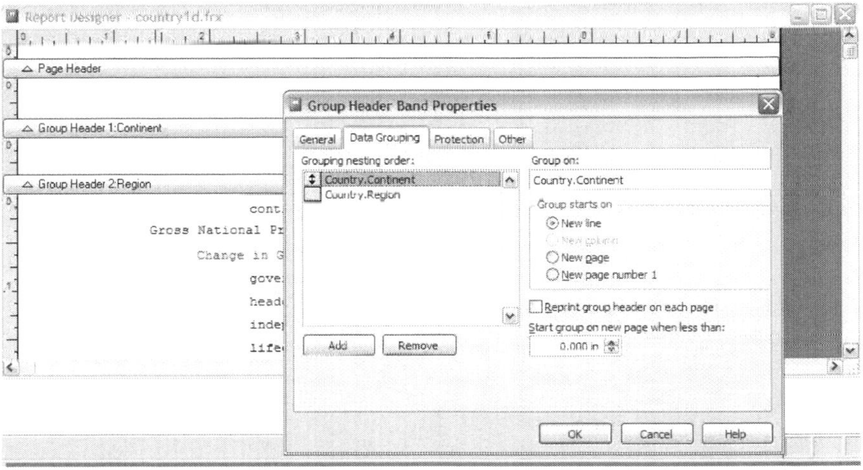

Figure 25. Group bands appear in the report layout.

Now that you have group bands available, move the associated data elements (Continent and Region into these bands).

You can add more layout elements to further indicate the group changes. In Figure 26, I've added a horizontal line to the outer group, and changed the font characteristics for group elements to distinguish them in the layout.

Now these layout controls repeat only when the group expressions change. You no longer have to use Print When to handle repeated instances in the detail band.

This report design isn't particularly pretty, but it gives you a good idea of what you can do with data groups in your layout. This ability helps you fulfill not only the requirements of repeated data in a "flat" or denormalized table, such as the World table, but also the requirements of multiple tables in a normalized data relationship.

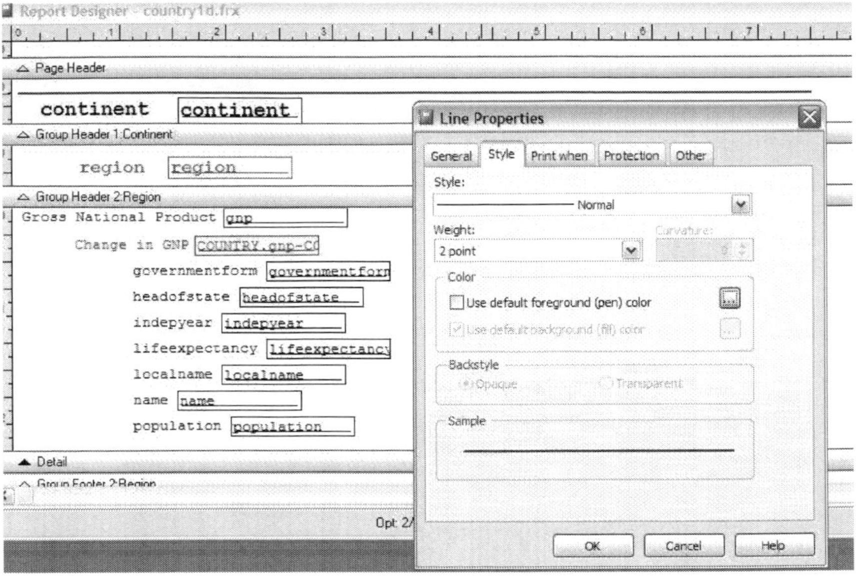

Figure 26. Add report content to group bands.

5.2 Handle multiple tables from your database

So far, all the reports you've designed handle data only from the Country table.

The World database, however, contains three tables: Country, CountryLanguage, and City. The CountryLanguage and City tables are related to the Country table through their CountryCode foreign key columns. Figure 27 shows the World database tables as they appear when examined in different applications.

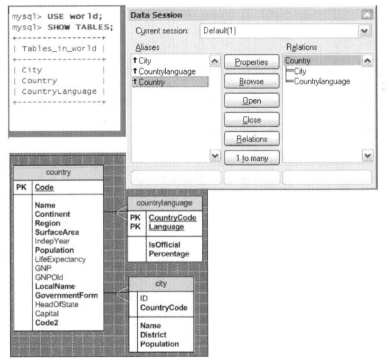

Figure 27. World data from a MySQL command line interface, in the VFP Data Session Window, and as a Visio diagram.

You have probably realized that you can create more complex reports in VFP simply by using more complex SQL statements than you've used so far in this tutorial.

For example, you might use a statement like this as your **SelectCmd** attribute for a cursoradapter, further de-normalizing the Country and City tables into a single, flattened cursor:

```
SELECT CAPITAL, CONTINENT, GNPOLD, GOVERNMENTFORM,
HEADOFSTATE, INDEPYEAR,LIFEEXPECTANCY, LOCALNAME,
CO.NAME, REGION, SURFACEAREA,CI.DISTRICT AS
CTY_DISTRICT, CI.NAME AS CTY_NAME, CI.POPULATION
AS CTY_POP, CI.ID AS CTY_ID FROM COUNTRY CO INNER
JOIN CITY CI ON CO.CODE = CI.COUNTRYCODE ORDER BY
CONTINENT, REGION, LOCALNAME,CTY_NAME
```

This SELECT statement exploits the one-to-many relationship between the Country and City tables. The data rows you fetch in the resulting cursor have many Country columns repeated throughout the multiple City records related to each Country.

Using either the Print When techniques or grouping techniques you used earlier, you can arrange this data to show the relationship in a meaningful way.

However, there are some limitations in this approach. For example, VFP does not allow more than 255 columns in the joined SELECT statement. This limitation is absolute, and it provides one good reason to question any decision to denormalize, or flatten, all data into a single table. Another good reason is the obvious inefficiency. When you denormalize your data and repeat data, you are pulling much more data across the network than you need to pull.

The SELECT statement you see above also contains more than 255 characters. There is also a limit of 255 characters when you assign a string to a variable in VFP, which applies to expressions you type in the Properties Window.

Unlike the number of columns, the Properties Window limit is not insurmountable, although it is annoying.

If you have a long SelectCmd value, break it up into smaller chunks with each chunk delimited (using square brackets or quotation marks), similar to what you did in the Command Window. Assign this value to the SelectCmd attribute of the appropriate cursoradapter object, in the OpenTables method of the DataEnvironment, like this:

```
THIS.CursorAdapter1.SelectCmd = [SELECT
CAPITAL, CONTINENT, GNPOLD, ] +
[GOVERNMENTFORM, HEADOFSTATE,
INDEPYEAR,LIFEEXPECTANCY, LOCALNAME, ]+
[CO.NAME, REGION, SURFACEAREA,CI.DISTRICT AS
CTY_DISTRICT, ] + [CI.NAME AS CTY_NAME,
CI.POPULATION AS CTY_POP, CI.ID ] + [AS CTY_ID
```

```
FROM COUNTRY CO INNER JOIN CITY CI ON ] +
[CO.CODE = CI.COUNTRYCODE ORDER BY CONTINENT,
REGION, LOCALNAME,CTY_NAME]
```

Be careful to include spaces between words, so the SQL statement will be correct when the parts of the string are concatenated.

You can break up this and other long statements into multiple lines, using semi-colons for readability. I have done this in a sample report file named BIGCOUNTRY.FRX, generated as a Quick Report, which uses this code.

You learn more about writing more useful code in methods of the Data Environment of a report shortly. In a later section of this tutorial, you'll also discover that you have more convenient ways to write such code, in a VFP class library.

You will find it extremely difficult to create appropriate CursorSchema values for long SQL statements, which are also subject to the Properties length restriction. Since CursorSchema is only a helpful design feature, not a report requirement you don't have to use it; you can specify your column names directly in report expressions instead.

You would probably like a convenient shortcut to make all these expressions available in a report design, when you can't use CursorSchema for all the fields. Here's how I generated BIGCOUNTRY.FRX:

First, I assigned the value of the SELECT statement to a variable in the Command Window, breaking it up into chunks because it was longer than 255 characters, like this:

```
x = "SELECT CAPITAL, CONTINENT, GNPOLD,
GOVERNMENTFORM, HEADOFSTATE,
INDEPYEAR,LIFEEXPECTANCY, LOCALNAME, CO.NAME,
REGION, SURFACEAREA,CI.DISTRICT AS
CTY_DISTRICT, CI.NAME AS CTY_NAME, " +
"CI.POPULATION AS CTY_POP, CI.ID AS CTY_ID
FROM COUNTRY CO INNER JOIN CITY CI ON CO.CODE
= CI.COUNTRYCODE WHERE CO.NAME='Germany' ORDER
BY CONTINENT, REGION, LOCALNAME,CTY_NAME "
```

Notice the **WHERE** *clause in the code above. It doesn't matter what WHERE clause you use, any small set of records will do. You just want to create a small cursor with appropriate data column definitions for your report design session.*

You need sample records to show VFP what the data will look like; a WHERE clause that provides no records (such as WHERE 1=2) will provide an empty cursor but less information about the data -- and no possibility of previewing your report while you design.

Next, I executed this statement from the Command Window, using a SQL handle I gathered in the usual way, and specifying the alias I wanted for the data in this report:

? SQLEXEC(1, x, "Country")

With the cursor available in my design environment I generated a Quick Report using "Form-style" layout instead of the default Columnar layout, to make sure I would have room for all the columns in my cursor. You can do this from the Command Window or by creating a new report and choosing Quick Report:

CREATE REPORT BigCountry FROM Country FORM

I used this Quick Report as a "head start" on report design, rearranging various report layout controls as needed.

*Then I added a cursoradapter to the Data Environment, but this time I added only the **Alias** and **UseDEDataSource** attribute values.*

*I left the **CursorSchema** attribute value at its unhelpful default (f1 c(10)), since I would not be using it, and I did not specify a **SelectCmd** attribute value since I could not specify it properly for this report. Instead, I added the equivalent OpenTables code for the Data Environment, as shown above.*

Beyond string limitations, and beyond the clumsiness of workarounds they force you to use, and even beyond performance considerations, VFP offers additional compelling incentives to bring multiple cursor results into your report's Data Environment. Once you bring the data in, you can use additional data manipulation within VFP to take advantage of many VFP optimizations and special reporting features.

In this section, you begin to use multiple cursors in relationship, so you can leverage these features.

First, you learn how to create and relate the multiple cursors in Visual Fox-Pro's Command Window, with a comparison to how you would perform the same task directly in MySQL. Then you learn how to use the related VFP cursors in a report. As you have done previously in this tutorial, after you learn the basic techniques, you learn to repeat the techniques for reporting purposes, without repeating the basic work each time you use them.

MySQL To give yourself a fresh start at this time, or at any time in your practice sessions, you may want to clear out any current data connections or open cursor in your environment, using two commands discussed earlier in the Command Window:

SQLDISCONNECT(0)

CLOSE DATA

To remove any variables that you might have created in the environment, add the following command:

CLEAR ALL

5.3 Relate multiple cursors in the VFP environment

As before, construct an appropriate connection string and use it to get a connection handle to MySQL. This time, for convenience, store the connection handle in a variable, so you can use it later:

myHandle= SQLSTRINGCONNECT(myString)

MySQL Notice that you store this integer value the same way you stored the string value earlier. Visual FoxPro is not a strongly-typed language. You do not need to declare the type of the variable before using it.

As you've seen in the examples, you do not even need to create or declare the variable before using it; the variable is created implicitly when you assign the value.

When you create a variable by assigning it a value in the Command Window, as you're doing here, the variable automatically has PUBLIC (global, in PHP) scope. In later sections of this tutorial, you see variables declared explicitly, with different scopes.

The last time you executed a query using SQLEXEC from the VFP Command Window, you included a third argument, the alias for the cursor of results the command fetches from MySQL. Issue the same command now, this time using your variable containing the connection handle:

SQLEXEC(myHandle,"SELECT * FROM COUNTRY ORDER BY Continent, Region ", "Country")

If you check the Data Session Window, you see the cursor is available with your designated alias, not the default alias **Sqlresult** you saw earlier. Now you can issue another SQLEXEC statement, using your handle and a different alias, to fetch a cursor holding data from the City table:

SQLEXEC(myHandle,"SELECT * FROM CITY ", "City")

In this SELECT statement, I have not included an ORDER BY clause, because, in the report, the order of the child cursor, City, is determined by its relationship to the parent cursor (Country) records. If this SELECT statement has an ORDER BY clause, the report will still function, but you have added time to the server's work, for no gain.

If you have used MySQL's Query Browser tool, you may know that it has a "master-detail" mode, which allows you to display multiple, scrollable sets of records in relation. (Refer to http://www.mysql.com/products/query-browser/tutorials/master-detail.html or http://dev.mysql.com/doc/query-browser/en/mysql-query-browser-using-masterdetail.html for details.) To determine the relationship between the two queries in the Query Browser, you use a dynamic parameter in the detail, or child, query, using the syntax **WHERE c.Country = :Code**, as shown in Figure 28 below. The dynamic parameter references the current value of the master, or parent, query's key value (the code column), and pulls the appropriate records in the child table for that value.

In the status bar at the bottom of the figure, you notice that the child result set is only 14 rows at the moment. When the user scrolls to another record in the parent, a new subset of City is fetched for the current Country record.

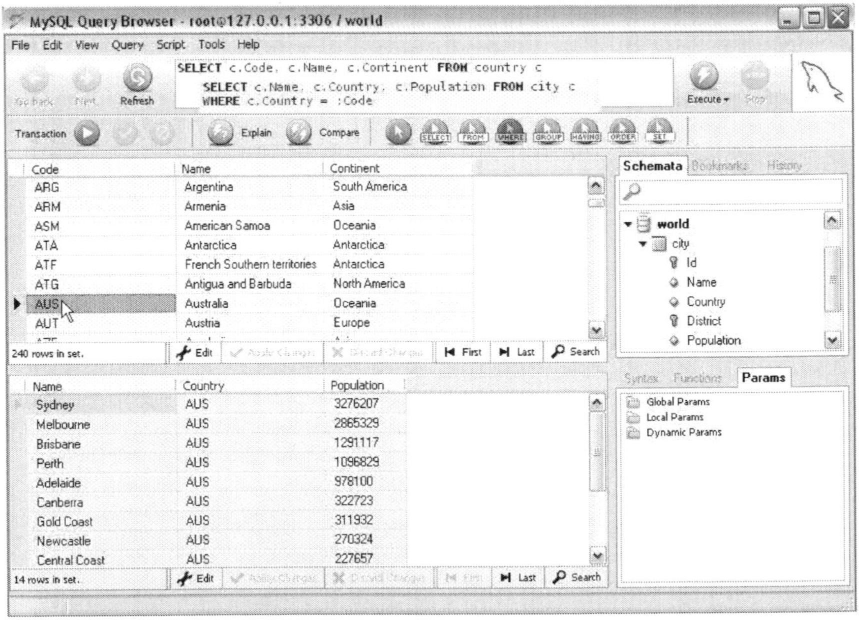

Figure 28. Master-detail relationships in the MySQL Query Browser.

You can use parameterized queries in Visual FoxPro also, and in some situations (such as editing the invoices for one customer), this is an appropriate approach. The VFP syntax for placing the dynamic parameter into the query is a little different; it uses a "**?**" instead of the "**:**". For example, if you want just the City records in the current Country row, and assuming that Country is the alias you have used for the parent cursor, you can issue this query:

SQLEXEC(myHandle, "SELECT * FROM CITY C WHERE C.CountryCode = ?Country.Code", "City")

You can also prepare and pre-compile this parameterized query, using the SQLPREPARE() statement, and then issue the SQLEXEC(myHandle) statement repeatedly, without the embedded SELECT statement, to refresh the contents of the City cursor as you move to different Country records. In later sections of the tutorial, you'll see additional ways of adjusting your query dynamically.

But for many reports, where you are interested in all the parent records, and therefore all the child records as you move through the various parent records, making these repeated, dynamic queries is not an efficient approach. Visual FoxPro offers you the alternative of fetching all the records at once and creating an indexed relation on the results. This technique ties the two, fully-populated, cursors together dynamically and does not require repeated fetches.

> *You may be surprised to hear that fetching all the records is more efficient than repeated queries. However, Visual FoxPro handles cursors, even very large cursors, using extremely performance-aware strategies. For example, VFP dynamically determines whether it should hold the full cursor in memory or swap portions to a cache on disk. You do not have to worry about any of the details or set any options to ensure this behavior.*

You use indexed relations by issuing two instructions to VFP:

Create an index on the child cursor. The index tells VFP what field, or what expression (for instance, two concatenated fields' values), represents the foreign key in the child table. In the City table, this expression is the Country-Code field. The index expression should be equivalent to the left side of the dynamic WHERE expression you would use in MySQL.

The index is a separate temporary file, which VFP builds very quickly. It provides an extremely fast way for VFP to move to the correct child cursor records as required by the relation.

Set the relation between the two cursors, from the parent to the child, using a field or fields from the parent table to indicate what data ties the two cursors together.

The field or fields from the parent table should be equivalent to the right side, or dynamic parameter, for the WHERE expression you would use in MySQL.

Here is the syntax you use, in the Command Window, to accomplish this task. On each line, the information beginning with **&&** is an in-line comment, not part of the command:

```
SELECT City            && see the note below
INDEX ON CountryCode TAG Temp
   * index on child cursor expression

SELECT Country

SET RELATION TO Code INTO City
   * set relation on parent cursor expression
```

You notice that the INDEX line contains the clause **TAG Temp**. *The index you create in this statement is temporary, because the cursor itself is temporary. VFP disposes of the index automatically when you close the cursor. The name you supply after the TAG keyword (here,* **Temp**) *does not matter, as long as it is a short name (10 characters or less), and also follows standard VFP/PHP variable naming requirements.*

The INDEX expression can include a concatenated expression, as indicated earlier. You may want to do this even when you don't have a concatenated foreign key. For example, in the World database, you could INDEX the City cursor ON the expression CountryCode+Name. Now the City records are ordered alphabetically by name in the report, within each group of Country-related records.

By default, VFP performs an inexact comparison of this expression and the parent key value, stopping when the length of the key value is exceeded, so the relationship between Country.Code and this expression works. (If you don't like this behavior, you can remove it by using the command SET EXACT ON. You can also override it for individual comparisons.)

You can use the TRANSFORM() expression and other casting or conversion functions in your index tag, to include non-string data in the index order. For instance, you might want to order the City values by population within each Country group.

After you execute these commands, open the Data Session Window. It looks similar to the Data Session Window in Figure 29.

Highlight each cursor in the Data Session list, and press the BROWSE button. When you scroll through the records in the Country browse window, you see the same behavior you saw in the MySQL Query Browser's Master-Detail view: only the relevant records in the City browse window appear. If you select the City alias, however, and check the status bar, you see that all City records are still in the cursor; unlike the MySQL Query Browser, VFP is not executing another SELECT statement against the City table every time you move to another record in the Country table.

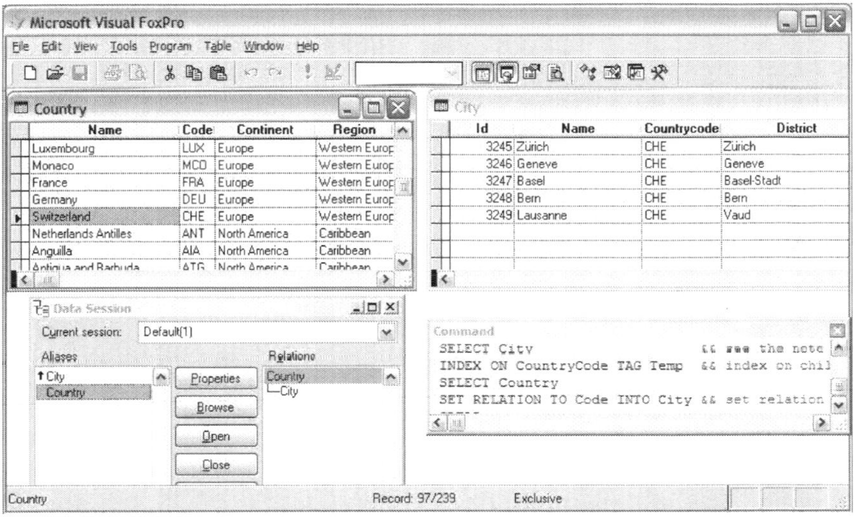

Figure 29. Related cursors in the VFP IDE.

In the code you used above, to create the index and relation, the SELECT statements are not SQL SELECT statements. They are FoxPro's way of setting the current focus to a particular cursor or table before taking action on it.

You perform the same task, setting focus to a cursor, when you highlight each cursor's name in the Data Session Window or click on that cursor's browse window in the VFP IDE.

When you set the InitiallySelectedAlias property in a Data Environment, you are performing this task as well, for use during the report. In other words, you are setting focus to a specific cursor on which the Report Engine acts. The Report Engine always processes a report by moving through the records in a single table or cursor, no matter how many cursors or tables are currently open and available. The InitiallySelectedAlias tells the Report Engine which cursor should drive the report.

> *In this tutorial, and in the VFP documentation, references to the driving alias for a report are always equivalent to the InitiallySelectedAlias for that report, if you set one in the report's Data Environment.*

5.4 Relate from the child to the parent

You can reverse the relation, by performing a similar set of steps. You don't need to re-fetch the cursors; everything you need is available for this new "view" of your data.

First, set the selected or driving alias to the Country cursor and remove the existing relation between Country and City. Then, set an index on the appropriate field (Code) in the Country cursor. Last, express the new relationship between City and Country:

```
SELECT Country

SET RELATION TO && remove the existing relation

INDEX ON Code Tag Temp

SELECT City

SET RELATION To CountryCode INTO Country
```

After you execute these five commands, you may have to close the City browse and re-open it to refresh its contents. After you do so, you can scroll through the City browse and see exactly one related record in the Country browse for each City (see Figure 30).

For what reason might you relate the records in this direction? Suppose you wanted to create a report on City records. You could easily perform the required join in a SELECT statement, attaching the name of the parent Country to each City record, denormalizing the data. But this action may require you to pull more data over the network than necessary; for example, the name "Germany" may be repeated in every one of 45 City rows.

As a more practical example, suppose you create a report of invoice totals, and wish to attach Customer data for each invoice. You don't want to repeat the Customer details (name, address, etc cetera) in one SELECT statement if you don't need to.

In either example, the difference becomes even clearer if you use grouping in reports. If your City report groups on Country, or your Invoice report groups on Customer, then you are only displaying the parent information once for every group. Meanwhile, if you created the join in your single SELECT statement, you have fetched the parent details for every single City or Invoice row.

It is a much better idea to fetch the parent cursor separately, as a "lookup" table. Your City report can group on City.CountryCode (or your Invoice report can group on Invoice.CustomerCode). With the relation set from child to parent, your parent data is available when you need it, in each group header or footer.

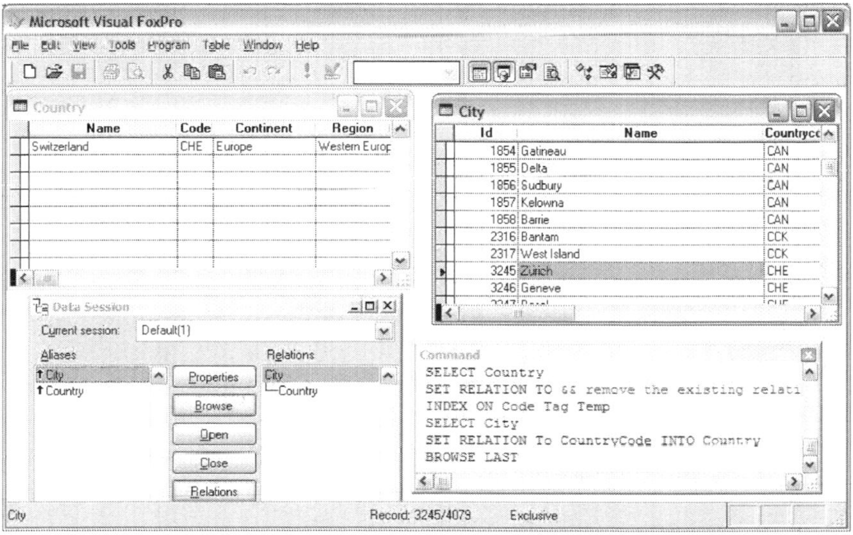

Figure 30. Reversing the relationship; browsing City records related to parent Country records.

5.5 Use multiple cursors in a VFP report

Because you've been prefacing all your cursor expressions in reports with their alias, you already have most of the ground work necessary to use multiple cursors in a report. With the relations set between child and parent, as they are in Figure 30, you only need to preface some expressions with the City alias, and others with the Country alias, for everything to work exactly as planned.

Almost exactly as planned. Such a report works as planned if you create the relations and indexes outside the report, and then run the report. Many people create VFP applications that work this way. However, if you want the report to set up these conditions automatically, without external lines of code, you need to tell the report about the relationships and indexes.

To begin preparing a multiple-cursor report sample, I started with **Country1b.frx**, the second report in this tutorial. In this report, you remember, you "improved" the Data Environment settings by removing the connection information from the cursoradapter object and attaching them to the DataEnvironment object containing the cursoradapter. Once the DataEnvironment holds the connection information, it can be shared by multiple cursors.

> *Notice that I have spelled the word both as "Data Environment" (with a space) and "DataEnvironment" (without a space).*
>
> *The term is used inconsistently in VFP documentation. However, in general, the term "Data Environment" refers to the Designer and layout surface while the single word "DataEnvironment" refers to an object, or instance of a class, available in VFP when you execute code. You learn more about the DataEnvironment class, shortly.*

Now it's time to make use of that information. I saved this report to a new name, **City**, to begin work.

The report's Data Environment starts with connection information, and one cursoradapter, with the alias Country. Add a second cursoradapter to the Data Environment and adjust the following attributes, similar to what you did for the first cursoradapter in this report:

- Set its **Alias** attribute value to **City**.

- Set its **UseDeDataSource** attribute value to **.T. - True**.

- Set its **SelectCmd** attribute to the following SELECT statement:
  SELECT CITY.Name, CITY.District, CITY.CountryCode, CITY.Population FROM CITY INNER JOIN COUNTRY CO ON CITY.CountryCode = CO.Code ORDER BY CO.Continent, CO.Region, CO.Name, CITY.District, CITY.Name
  Notice that I used the ORDER BY clause in this statement. I plan to make City the **InitiallySelectedAlias** for the report, and group on the values you see in this ORDER BY clause.
  Notice, also, that some of these ORDER BY values come from the Country table, and that the two tables are joined in this query. Although I chose not to fetch the repeated Country data columns into this cursor for reasons of performance, I can still join the tables for any work I really want the database to do for me.

- To give the Report Designer appropriate information, set the **Cursor-Schema** attribute to the following value:

```
Name C(33), CountryCode C(3), District C(20),
Population I
```

The report's Data Environment should now contain your second cursoradapter. Returning your attention to the Properties Window, change the **InitiallySelectedAlias** attribute of the DataEnvironment object to the value **City**.

Finally, change the **SelectCmd** attribute of the Country cursor to include the Code column, since you didn't use it before. You need the Code column, this time, for the relation. You don't need to add information about the Code column to the **CursorSchema** attribute value, since this attribute's description of the report contents is used solely for design purposes and you don't plan to use this column in the report output.

You can also drop any columns you don't need in this report from the Country **SelectCmd**, as well as removing the ORDER BY clause. It's a good idea to eliminate fetching columns, or other SQL work, that you don't need.

Again, it doesn't matter if the **CursorSchema** attribute value for the Country cursor exactly matches the new **SelectCmd** value for this cursor. However, be sure to remove any layout controls containing expressions that use columns no longer in your SELECT statement from the report layout, since they are not available to the report engine when you run the report.

In your sample code, I used the following **SelectCmd** for `City.frx` and adjusted the layout to contain only these fields from the Country table:

```
select Continent, LocalName, Name, Region, Code
from country
```

So far, you have not given any relationship instructions. Before you do so there is still one more thing you need to do to make this report "safe for multiple cursors". If you drag and drop any field from the City cursor into the report layout at this point, and try to preview the report, you receive the error "alias City not found". What's wrong?

The error that is really occurring underneath, as the report's Data Environment tries to open your cursors, is "Connection is busy". Because you are now sharing the connection between cursors, you must ensure that the first cursor is fully fetched before VFP tries to open the second one.

To avoid this issue, you could use multiple connections for each cursor in a report – but this isn't really necessary, and is not the most efficient strategy for many database servers. Instead, set the value of the **FetchSize** attribute for both cursoradapter objects to **-1**. This value indicates you want all records to be fetched. The FetchSize value defaults to **100**, which isn't practical for reports.

When you've set FetchSize for both cursoradapters, the Properties Window for your City cursoradapter object should resemble the one in Figure 31, which has been set to the **Non-Default Properties Only** view.

The Properties Window help information, at the bottom of the panel, informs you that the instructions in FetchSize are subject to limitation based on the value of another attribute, MaxRecords. Since MaxRecords defaults to -1 (All records), however, you don't need to worry about it.

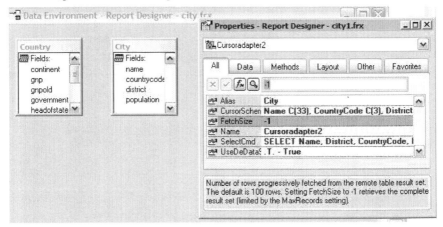

Figure 31. The City cursoradapter for a report.

If you are experienced with MySQL, you may know that it is possible to execute multiple statements in a single command, separated by semi-colons.

This capability was first implemented in version 4.1 of the MySQL ODBC driver. You can get the details, including additional configuration requirements, here http://dev.mysql.com/doc/mysql/en/connection-parameters.html.

Using the CLIENT_MULTI_STATEMENTS option with driver version 4.1 and above might resolve the "connection is busy" issue in some cases, but I have chosen not to include this capability in my instructions. Many MySQL users do not use this version of the driver yet, and some are using the database on hosted web servers (so they don't have the option to upgrade). Also, including the multiple SQL statements in one SQL execution, while perfectly legal in VFP, is not as intuitive as attaching each SELECT statement to an associated cursoradapter object in the Data Environment.

Having made the change to FetchSize, you can go on to set your relations for the report. In this initial version, you just transfer the code you wrote in the Command Window to the report, using the following steps:

Double-click anywhere on the Country cursoradapter object in the Data Environment Designer window. This action brings up a code snippet edit, with two drop downs at the top (see Figure 32). The left-hand dropdown is set to **Cursoradapter1** (the object that has the alias Country at runtime). Change the right-hand dropdown to access the **AfterCursorFill** event, which appears pre-filled with an LPARAMETERS line. Below the LPARAMETERS line, type the same code you used in the Command Window:

SELECT Country

INDEX ON Code Tag Temp

Double-click anywhere on the City cursoradapter object in the Data Environment Designer window. Using the right-hand dropdown for this object, navigate to the same **AfterCursorFill** event. Below the LPARAMETERS line, type the appropriate code for the City-Country relationship:

SELECT City

SET RELATION To CountryCode INTO Country

Figure 32. Writing Index and Relation code for a report's DataEnvironment object container.

Save the report. Now you're ready to adjust the report layout to use both cursors, and leverage the relationship.

In your sample code, I have adjusted **City.FRX** to include group levels appropriate to the columns on which I ordered the City cursor. Because the relationship exists, I am able to use any of the columns in the Country cursor and know that, as the report engine moves through the City cursor serving as the main cursor (or "driving alias") for this report, the current values in the Country cursor are appropriate to the current row of the City cursor. In Figure 33, you can see a group levels on Continent, Country name, and Country region. The group header band associated with the Country name expression features a layout control using the expression **ALLTRIM(COUNTRY.name) + " (" + ALLTRIM(COUNTRY.localname) + ") "**. As you can see, this data must come from the Country cursor; the localname column was not even used in the ORDER BY clause for the City cursor. Figure 34 shows you the results.

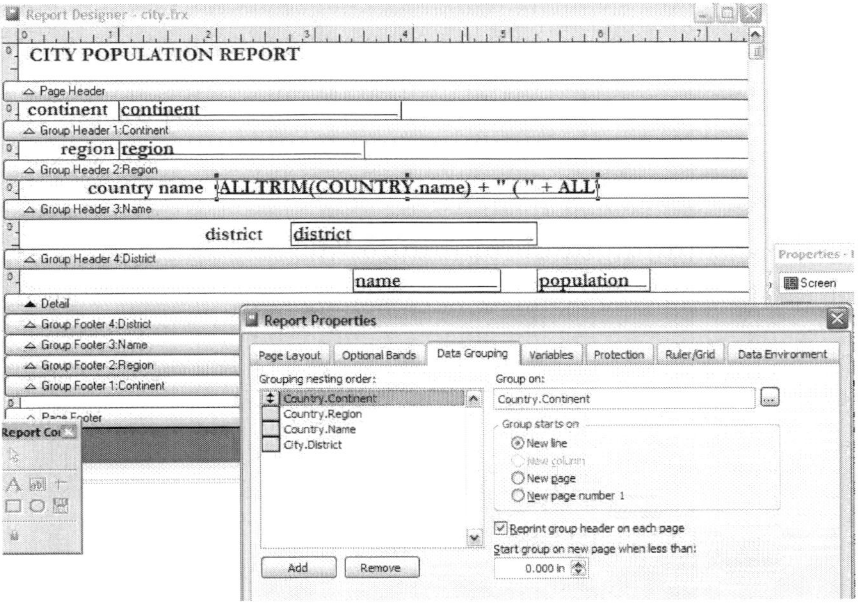

Figure 33. *Leveraging related cursors in a report design...*

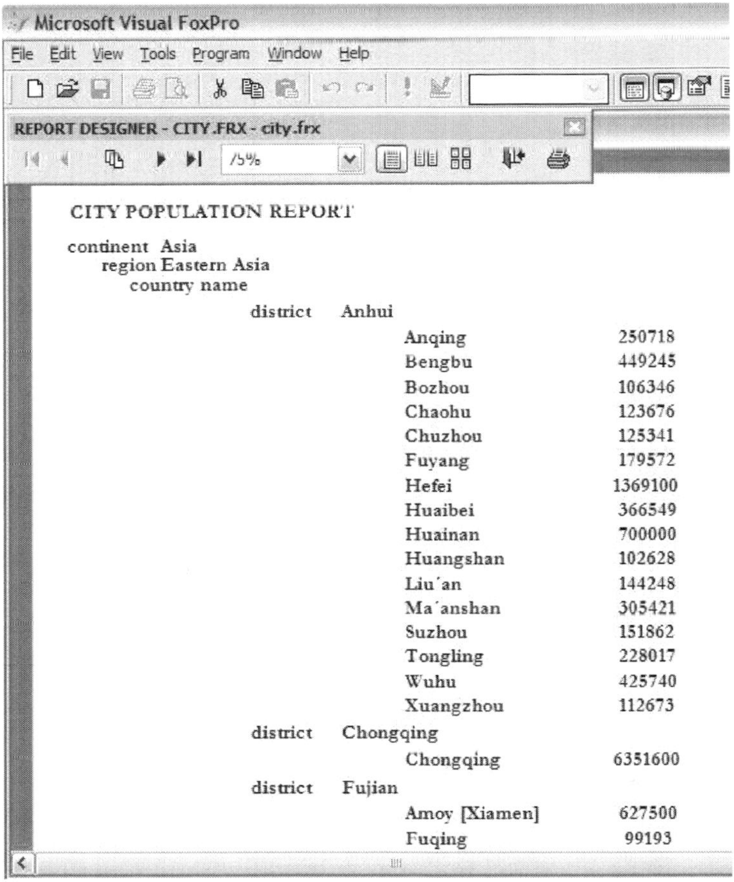

Figure 34. ...Leveraging related cursors in report results.

5.6 Use multiple detail bands for multiple parent-child relationships

Fetching the parent data as a lookup table in this way is efficient for the City report. But, to fully appreciate what you can do with multiple cursors in a VFP report, you must reverse the relationship again: drive the report, and the relationship from Country to City.

Consider the World database structure, shown in Figure 27, again. As you know, the Country table has two child tables: City and CountryLanguage.

Suppose you wanted to create a report on Country records that showed all re-lated City records and also all related CountryLanguage records? You could do this with a single cursor, but, because there is no relationship between City and CountryLanguage, and the joins are not straightforward. To "flatten" or denormalize this data into a single cursor would require outer joins to both child tables and result in a great deal of wasted space in the rows.

Using cursors in VFP, you can resolve this dilemma very simply; you can set up multiple relations from the parent to child tables. The SET RELATION command you have already used can include a list of child tables in one command, or it can be used multiple times with an ADDITIVE clause, to ac-cumulate relationships.

In your next report, you leverage this ability and also assign each child table its own detail band layout.

To begin the next report, which I named **World.Frx** in your samples, I created a new report and then used the **Load Data Environment** option on the Report menu to import the data connection and cursor information from **Country1b.frx**. (Refer to Figure 18.) This gave me the basic data setup for the report's driving alias cursor, and the appropriate InitiallySelectedAlias (**Country**).

Assuming you have done the same, you now adjust the Country cur-soradapter object in your report, by setting its **FetchSize** attribute value to **-1** and by adding the Code column to the SELECT statement in the **SelectCmd** attribute.

Add two additional cursoradapter objects, one with the alias **City** and one with the alias **CountryLanguage**. Besides the alias attribute, you edit attrib-utes for these two objects with which you are already familiar. Each cur-soradapter object receives non-default values for the following attributes:

- In **SelectCmd**:
  select CountryCode, IsOfficial, Language, Percentage from countrylanguage
  and
  select CountryCode,Name,Population from city

- In **CursorSchema**
  COUNTRYCODE C(3), ISOFFICIAL C(1), LANGUAGE C(25), PERCENTAGE B(2)
  and
  COUNTRYCODE C(3), NAME C(33), POPULATION I

- In **UseDEDataSource**: .T.- True

- In **Fetchsize**: **-1**

Finally, add code for both indexes and relations into the **AfterCursorFill** event of the third cursoradapter object. Since at this stage of the report initialization process all three objects are available, it is a convenient point at which to put all the code you need:

```
SELECT CountryLanguage
INDEX ON CountryCode TAG Temp
SELECT City
INDEX ON CountryCode TAG Temp
SELECT Country
SET RELATION TO Code INTO CountryLanguage, Code
INTO City
```

With the Data Environment prepared, turn your attention to the report layout.

First, create groups appropriate to the ORDER BY in my SELECT statement for Country, the driving alias for this report. This time, you can also add an inner group for Country.Code, as you can see in Figure 35. Although there should be only one Code value for each Country cursor record, this report contains multiple child records from City and CountryLanguage for each Country record.

> *Those of you who are VFP programmers may wonder why I did not use VFP's SET SKIP syntax, signifying a one-to-many relationship, when I wrote the code above to set up the relations. Later in this tutorial, I'll show you how to perform similar tasks using relation objects instead of SET RELATION code, but these examples may not necessarily use the equivalent OneToMany property of the relation object.*
>
> *The reason for this omission is simple: When you use the techniques provided here for to relate multiple cursors in a report, and if you do not indicate any one-to-many relationships, the report engine assumes this condition for all related child cursors for the duration of the report. If some of the relationships are actually one-to-one, this does no harm.*

Add information about each Country, from the first cursoradapter, into the innermost group header, by dragging and dropping a few fields. The layout is now ready for the addition of data from the child tables.

From the **Report** menu, select **Optional Bands...** .As you see in Figure 35, the dialog tab starts out with one detail band, the default. Press the **Add** button to add a second detail band. Press **OK** to return to the Report Designer layout window.

Figure 35. Beginning to add a detail band to a multi-cursor report.

The layout now contains two detail bands. Double-click on each detail band separator, and add an expression representing each of the child aliases in the **Target alias expression** input box you see in the Detail Band Properties dialog. As shown in Figure 36, because this value is an expression, you must enclose the literal alias value in quotation marks (either double or single). You can also check the **Associated header and footer bands** box, as I've done in your sample, to add some organizing information to each of the detail bands.

> *The value is an expression because Visual FoxPro programmers often generate the alias name at runtime. You can store a variable holding the dynamically-generated alias, rather than a delimited string, in this box.*

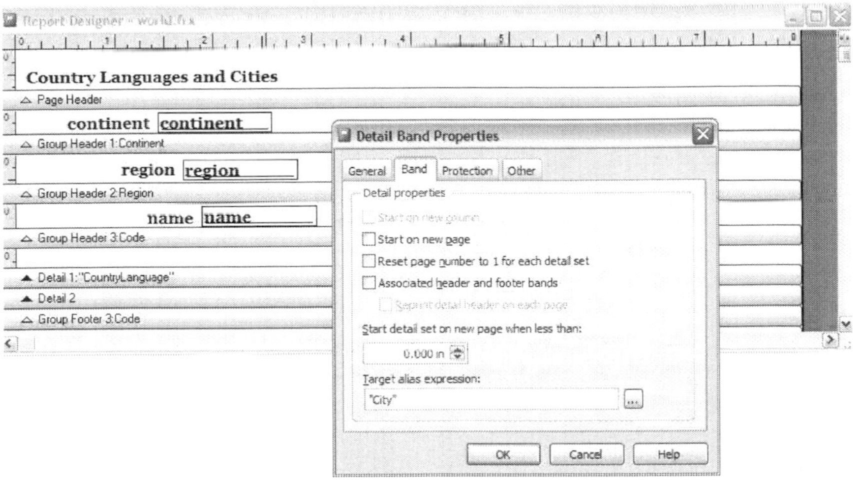

Figure 36. Adding a target alias expression.

When you've added both target alias values to the report, drag each detail band separate bar down to make room in the two detail bands. You can drag columns from each child cursor into each of the two detail bands from the Data Environment, as you've done previously. You can see the simple layout I prepared in your sample in Figure 37. I added the colors to help you distinguish between the content that comes from different report bands in the screen shots.

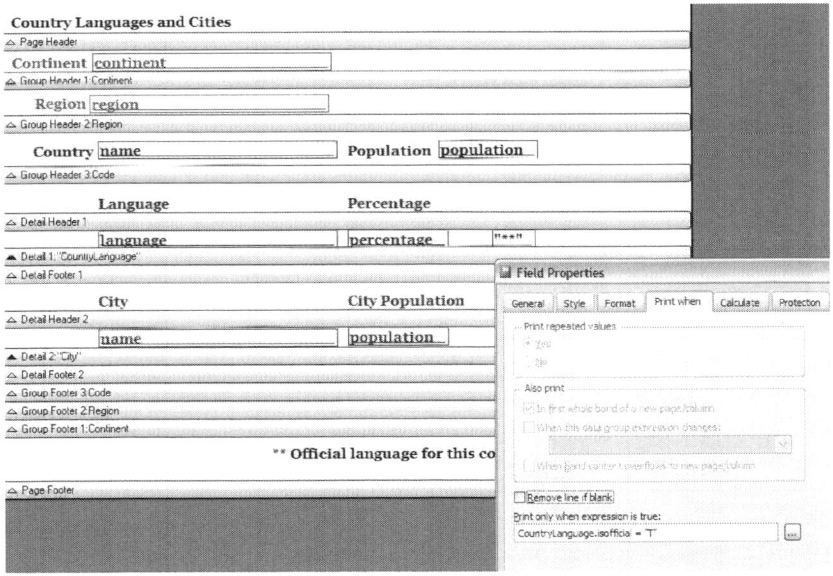

Figure 37. A completed multi-detail layout.

In your sample, I've added one column into the CountryLanguage detail band that deserves comment: in Figure 37, you see the expression "**"". The IsOfficial column in the CountryLanguage table is a single-character value, defaulting to "F", and indicating whether a language is the official language for a country. Rather than show the native values "T" or "F" in the report output, I chose to create an expression of two asterisks, and added the Print When expression `CountryLanguage.isofficial = "T"` to identify when this expression should appear in the report. I also added a "footnote" in the page footer, to explain what the asterisks meant when they appeared. The results appear in the report preview you see, at the end of this section, in Figure 41.

> *In this case, I could have used a label with the literal asterisks instead of an expression – labels and other VFP report layout controls, such as shapes, also support Print When.*

> *I tend to use expressions rather than labels, even when the expression is very simple. When you find you have more complex requirements, and must return to re-edit a report it is easier to edit the expression to have more complex contents later. If you substituted an expression for the label at that point, you may have to re-do your formatting work, Print When expressions, et cetera.*

Again, the report output in Figure 41 is not elegant; this report simply serves to introduce you to possibilities for manipulating data in a report, not format.

This is a good time to take a moment to look back to Figure 13, which previews the first report you designed. Notice the default .NULL. representation of the indepyear value for the record shown in the preview. Other data in this column appears suspect, at least in my copy of the World database; for example, the indepyear value for Japan is -660. The value may actually be correct, if Japan had a year of independence in 660 BCE (Before the Common Era), but it's not very helpful in the present form, so I'll choose to omit negative values for this report.

By now you must realize that you have many options for displaying this value more intelligently, using Print When expressions as well as other VFP facilities. Consider the following options:

Add a Print When expression for both the label and expression, indicating that they should not print at all when the value of the expression is null or when it is negative. You can express this condition in VFP as:

```
country.indepyear > 1AND NOT
ISNULL(country.indepyear)
```

As you see, this syntax is very similar to how you would express it in SQL. Since nothing else appears on the same horizontal line in the report, you can instruct the report to remove this line when the two layout controls do not print. I've done this by selecting both layout controls and using the **Properties** tab of the Multiple Selection dialog, in Figure 38.

Layer two controls on top of each other. One, with the Print When expression above, outputs the indepyear value. The other one, with the opposite expression (`country.indepyear < 1 OR ISNULL(country.indepyear)` outputs an alternative expression, such as "year not available".

Use the VFP IIF() ("immediate if" or "in-line if") expression to provide two alternative expressions in one control, for example:

```
IIF(COUNTRY.indepyear > 1 AND NOT
ISNULL(COUNTRY.indepyear),COUNTRY.indepyear,"year
not available").
```

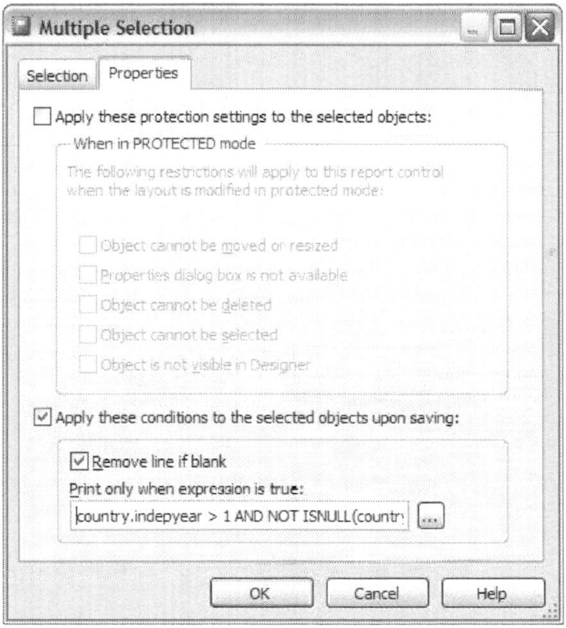

Figure 38. Print When expression for multiple objects, suppressing a line when they don't appear.

You find all these options included in a final variant of the first report, **Country1e**. I have removed some of the other detail band fields and added a second column to the report, using the Report Properties dialog's **Page Layout** panel, as shown in Figure 39, so you can compare "good" and "bad" indepyear values, side by side.

Because the new expressions sometimes require more width than the layout controls provide, I used the **Stretch with overflow** option for each of them, and also marked these controls and all controls further down in the detail band with the instruction to **Float** in the layout, when the output above stretches downwards. Using **Float** allows the band to adjust for the line that may be removed when blank as well as the new, stretching objects.

You can see the preview view of this report in Figure 40.

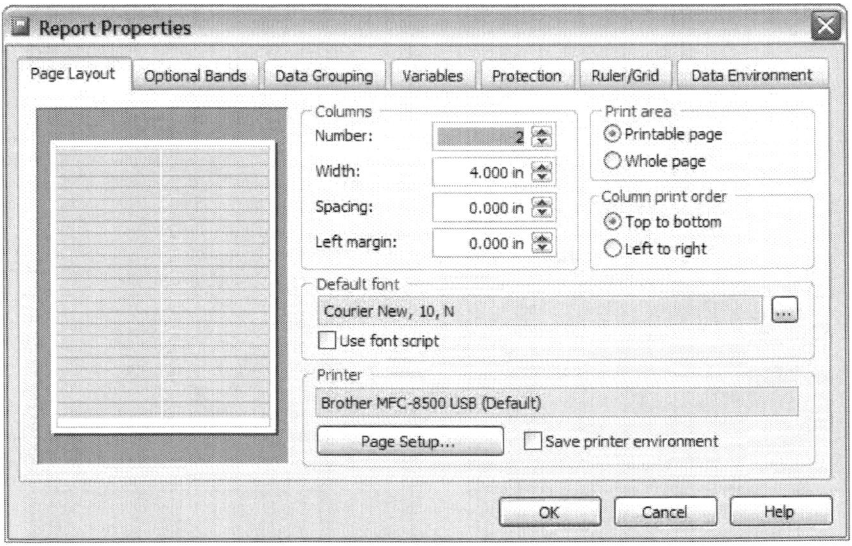

Figure 39. Add columns to a report using the Report Properties dialog.

REPORT DESIGNER - COUNTRY1E.FRX - country1e.frx - Page 1

```
              government form Special...
                 headofstate Jiang Zemin                              lifeexpectancy          01.00
original            indep year      year not         Gross National Product      1043.00
value: .NULL.     not available   available            Change in GNP            110.00
    lifeexpectancy               79.50                    government form Republic
                                                             headofstate Natsagiin...
                                                           indepyear               1921
Gross National Product    3787042.00                  original            1921              1921
    Change in GNP          -405596.00                 value: 1921
       government form Constitution...                                        67.30
          headofstate Akihito                            lifeexpectancy
original          indep year      year not
value: -660     not available   available            Gross National Product    256254.00
    lifeexpectancy               80.70                    Change in GNP         -7197.00
                                                          government form Republic
Gross National Product    982268.00                          headofstate Chen Shui-...
    Change in GNP          64549.00                        indepyear               1945
       government form People's Repu...               original            1945              1945
          headofstate Jiang Zemin                     value: 1945
original          indep year      year not                                    76.40
value: -1523    not available   available                lifeexpectancy
    lifeexpectancy               71.40
                                                          region    Middle...
```

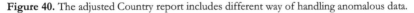

Figure 40. The adjusted Country report includes different way of handling anomalous data.

These options do not exhaust the possibilities, but they should give you some ideas.

Why does VFP give you so many different ways to handle the same data issue?

Data scenarios are practically infinite, and reporting display requirements extrapolated from data schemas are definitely infinite! VFP reports give you the options you need to handle whatever output results you need.

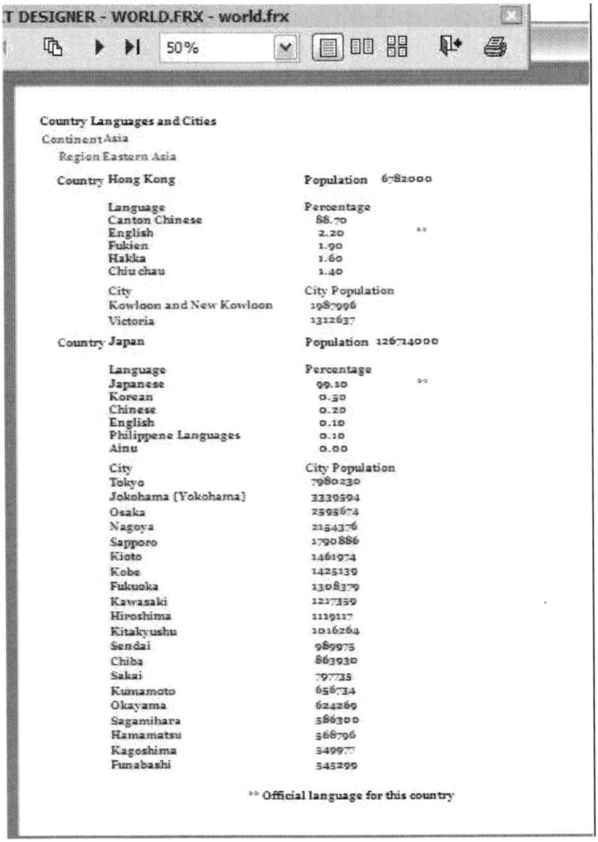

Figure 41. Multi-detail report preview.

5.7 Use multiple detail bands without data relationships

Normally, when you use multiple aliases in a report, the multiple cursors they represent are in some relationship to each other, whether many-to-one (as you saw in CITY.FRX) or one-to-many (as you saw in WORLD.FRX). This is the most common reason to use multiple detail bands. Occasionally, however, you might want to create a report on two sets of data that have no relationship – and you'll find multiple detail bands useful in this situation as well.

For example, you might use one cursor to pull details about a customer, and a second to pull all the contact addresses available for that customer. Because your SELECT statements already pre-selected the one customer record and its related address records, you don't really need the Report Engine's ability to handle the relationships. Because your report concerns only one record in the parent cursor, you don't really need more than one detail band in this case. You can put the customer data in either a group band or a page band.

I have created such a report, using one city and multiple languages, as ONECITY_MANYLANGUAGES.FRX, in your samples. The report has the following DataEnvironment characteristics:

The **InitiallySelectedAlias** for the DataEnvironment is **CountryLanguage.**

The first cursor's **Alias** attribute is set to **City** and its **SelectCmd** is **SELECT Name,CountryCode from city WHERE Name = 'Amsterdam'**.

The second cursor's **Alias** attribute is set to **CountryLanguage** and its SelectCmd is **SELECT Language from countrylanguage WHERE CountryCode = ?City.CountryCode**.

Refer to Figure 42 to see what this simple report looks like, in the Report Designer and in Preview. As you recall, the "?" in the second SelectCmd indicates that the value is a dynamic parameter, similar to the MySQL **:code** syntax you looked at earlier in this tutorial. Because the first cursoradapter already exists by the time the second query is run, this parameter is already available and automatically filled, similar to what you saw in the MySQL Query Browser.

> *Note that you could also have parameterized the first query (***SELECT Name,CountryCode from city WHERE Name = ?CityName***). Because VFP has no way to pull the value for this parameter by itself, it prompts for a value at runtime (see Figure 43, a report variant available in your sample files as PROMPTCITY_MANYLANGUAGES).*
>
> *In applications, you can pre-fill the parameter using additional code outside the report to create dynamic reports rather than storing the parameter value directly in the* **SelectCmd.** *You learn a flexible technique for filtering queries later in this tutorial.*

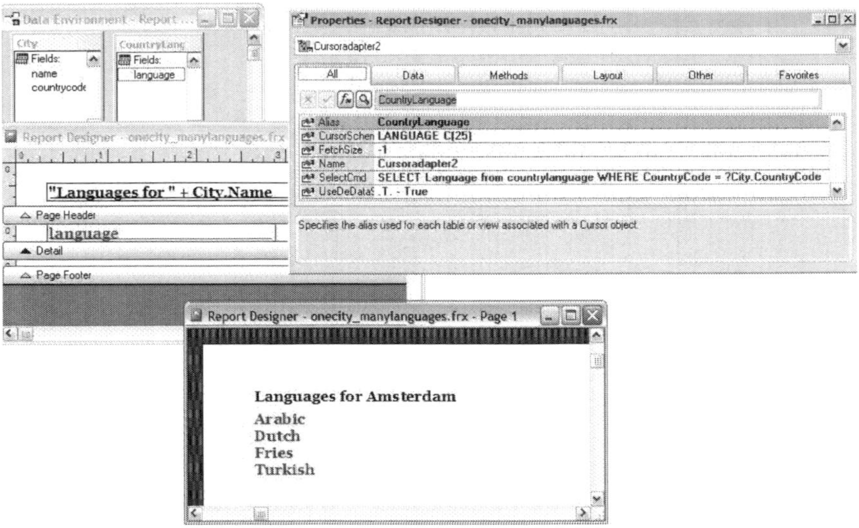

Figure 42. A simple parameterized query allows you to pull in detail in a second, unrelated cursor relying on a value from the first.

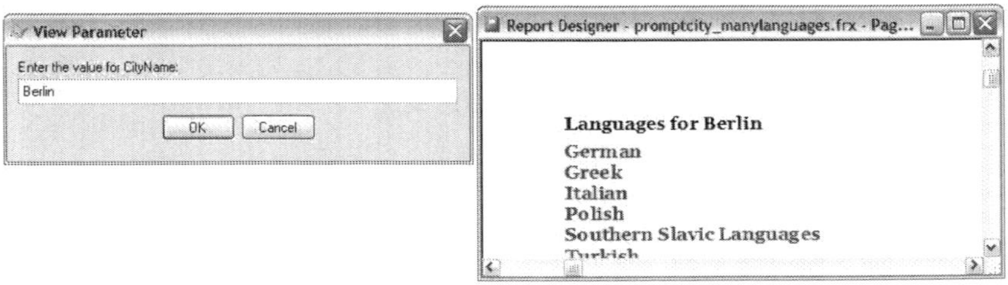

Figure 43. A prompt dialog occurs for a parameter VFP needs the user's help to initialize.

What if you have multiple records in multiple cursors, and you wish to display all the records in each cursor in turn? Fulfill this requirement following the steps described below.

> *You might expect that you can use multiple detail bands to do this, simply by assigning the appropriate* **Target alias** *for each cursor to each band.*
>
> *However, because the REPORT FORM command technically moves the record pointer in a single alias (the driving, or Initially Selected alias), the Report Engine ordinarily relies on relationships between cursors to figure out how to move the record pointers in other cursors.*
>
> *Without relationships, the Report Engine cannot evaluate group break expressions in multiple cursors with any confidence, because the current values in the un-selected cursors are arbitrary.*

- Set the Target alias for each band to the alias of the cursor you want in the first band.

- Set the **InitiallySelectedAlias** for the Data Environment to the same value.

- Attach some instructions to all additional detail bands (presumably, one for each additional unrelated cursor) to move the record pointer in the correct file yourself, and to make sure each band appears the correct number of times for the associated cursor.

I have included an example of this technique as UNRELATED_ WORLD.FRX in your samples. Although the report is simple, it gives you a generic version of the appropriate instructions that you can use with any data set.

In this example from the World database, you pull a set of all cities and all languages available in the database. You are not concerned with showing any relationship, such as how many people potentially speak each language, perhaps because this is a report for a directory or index table.

For brevity, I've limited the cities and languages to those beginning with the letter "T" in the sample Data Environment, as you might want to do if you were delivering a section of a directory.

> *In a real directory, you could create such a report with a dynamic parameter, delivering the cities and languages a letter at a time.*

> *If you ever need to do this, you can chain, or continue, multiple reports for the sequenced letters using the keyword NOPAGEEJECT. This keyword indicates that the reports are part of a continued sequence; it allows them to be treated as one print job, or displayed in one preview.*

I've also set up columns, to deliver more content in a more concentrated presentation. You'll see that the columns in this report flow "left to right", rather than "top to bottom", as they did in the first columnar report. (You'll find this setting in the Report Properties dialog.) When you examine the report, notice that objects in header and footer bands, such as the green line you can see in Figures 44 and 45 below, can stretch across all the columns; this is a very useful feature when you set the column flow "left to right".

Following the steps above, since the City cursor is displayed first in my sample report, I've used the expression **"City"** as the **Target alias** for each detail band. I've also set this cursor as my **InitiallySelectedAlias** for the report. The only remaining task to display the CountryLanguage records properly is to add some information in the Detail band dialog for the second detail band.

Previously, you've only used the **Band** tab in this dialog; now you need to switch to the **General** tab (to the left in the dialog). You add the following instruction to be executed **On exit** from this detail band, as shown in Figure 44:

UDF_GetDetails("city","countrylanguage")

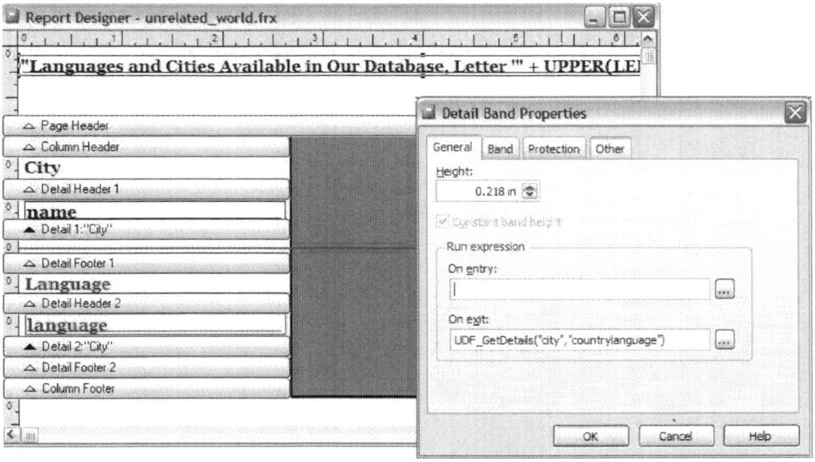

Figure 44. Adding a UDF with commands to your report.

UDF_GetDetails is a set of commands expressed as a user-defined function, similar to UDFs in both MySQL and SQL Server. VFP stores them in procedure or program files.

You'll find this UDF in a file named UDF_GetDetails.PRG in the directory holding sample reports (the PRG extension is the VFP default for "program"). It takes two arguments, which must be specified in correct sequence: the report's driving alias and the alias of the cursor you wish to display in this detail band. If this report had additional unrelated cursors in additional detail bands, you would use the same UDF for each one, changing the value in the second argument each time.

You don't need to understand how the UDF works, although you can use the **File Open...** dialog (choosing **Files of type Program**) to look at it. You can see the full contents of the UDF as well as the report results in Figure 45: First, all cities beginning with "F" are displayed and then (in red on Page 2 in the screen shot) all languages beginning with "F" are displayed.

Languages and Cities Available in Our Database, Letter 'F'

City			
Fagatogo	Florencio Varela	Forme	Feira
Francistown	Fortaleza		Foz d
Franca	Florianópolis		Franc
Ferraz de Vasconcelos	Francisco Morato		Firoza
Fuenlabrada	Faridabad		Fateh
Farrukhabad-cum-...	Faizabad		Ferrai
Firenze	Foggia		Funab
Forli	Fukuoka		Fukus
Fukuyama	Fujisawa		Fuchu
Fukui	Fuji		Fukav
Fujieda	Fujinomiya		Fuzho
Fujimi	Flying Fish Cove		Fosha
Fushun	Fuxin		Fuvan
Fengcheng	Fuyu		Fujin
Fuling	Fu'an		Florer
Fuqing	Floridablanca		Fort-é
Fianarantsoa	Fès		Ferna
Fresnillo	Faisalabad		Frank
Faaa	Focsani		Freet
Freiburg im Breisgau	Fürth		Frede
Fengshan	Fengyuan		Fargo
Fakaofo	Funafuti		Fort V
Fort Worth	Fresno		Fonta
Fremont	Fort Lauderdale		Fayett
Fullerton	Flint		Fall R
Fort Collins	Fairfield		

Language			
French	Fon	Ful	
Fang	Finnish	Fijian	
Faroese	Fukien	Friuli	
Fries	Fur	Futun	

```
udf_getdetails.prg

    LPARAMETERS tcDrivingAlias, tcTargetAlias
    IF NOT EOF(tcTargetAlias)
        SKIP 1 IN (tcTargetAlias)
        IF EOF(tcTargetAlias)
            SKIP -1 IN (tcTargetAlias)
            GO BOTTOM IN (tcDrivingAlias)
        ELSE
            SKIP -1 IN (tcDrivingAlias)
        ENDIF
    ENDIF
    RETURN
```

Figure 45. Unrelated cursors in the report.

You can add other commands to be executed in reports, for any band, both when a band begins processing and as it finishes processing. The **General** Tab of the Band Properties dialog, shown in Figure 44 for the Detail band, includes these features for each band type.

You have already learned that you can add also commands directly in the Data Environment, using code snippet windows.

The possibilities here are almost unlimited – and beyond the scope of this tutorial!

5.8 Move on to improving the process

This concludes your whirlwind tour of the data-centric capabilities of the VFP Report Designer. Although there's much more you can do with data in VFP reports – calculating summary values as part of report processing, for example – these additional capabilities do not have specific requirements for external data, and are well-presented in the Visual FoxPro documentation.

As you've worked on the last few reports, you've probably noticed that you perform many tasks repeatedly, such as setting FetchSize for each cursoradapter object. You also loaded a single Data Environment setup for one report to many reports requiring the same data. What would happen if you wanted to change a SELECT statement consistently, across these reports? You would need to open each report and make the relevant changes.

In the next installment of this tutorial, you learn about the object-oriented features that VFP provides to streamline your development process. With a good set of specialized tools, you can minimize the number of external-data-related tasks you repeat for multiple reports. You have such a toolset supplied as part of the source code for this tutorial.

Efficient applications start with a good set of tools, just as design sessions do. In the final installment of this tutorial, you go on to learn about report delivery: how you invoke reporting commands in applications, using a minimum of code and a generic process.

Chapter 6
Use objects to make the process repeatable

The first tool you need to improve your reporting process is a DataEnvironment you can create outside reports, and which you can attach to multiple reports. When the report runs, an instance of this class gives consistent behavior to all the reports. In this chapter, you learn how to create and subclass an appropriate DataEnvironment.

> *Earlier, when you used the Tools Options dialog, you saw that the new VFP reporting engine is labeled "object-assisted". However, the techniques you're going to learn in this section work with both report engines because, in fact, reports in VFP have always been assisted by an external DataEnvironment object. The new engine simply allows much more flexibility and the use of many other types of VFP objects during all phases of the reporting process.*

All classes in VFP are derived from a defined set of VFP base classes; the DataEnvironment is one VFP base class. The objects aggregated in a Data Environment container, such as cursoradapters and relations, are instances of other VFP base classes.

When you don't specify any class to use for a report, VFP uses base classes for all the Data Environment components. By creating a subclass or derived class in a VFP class library, you have the opportunity to fine-tune various aspects of the Data Environment object used for your reports, and to put inheritance to work.

> *If you are a PHP programmer, you are probably familiar with the concepts of object-oriented programming; if you are a Java or .Net programmer, you certainly are!*
>
> *Like these languages, VFP supports object inheritance and aggregation, although of course the syntax and some aspects of behavior are slightly different in each language.*
>
> *For example, VFP works differently from PHP when you override a method in a derived class. In VFP, you can augment a method, call "up" the inheritance chain, and deliberately trigger the code in a method on various levels of the class hierarchy to control the sequence. Also, although both languages have Try-Catch structured error handling, there are some differences in the way these constructs work.*
>
> *The set of classes supplied with this tutorial makes liberal use of VFP abilities and syntax. Thanks to inheritance, you won't have to understand the behavior to put my recommendations into practice. You simply derive your classes from the ones I've supplied, and add your data-specific elements, such as SELECT commands.*

6.1 Introducing your first VFP class library

A VCX class library is a separate file with the extension VCX. Like FRX files, VCX files have a companion file with the extension VCT.

To create your first VCX-based DataEnvironment class, open the sample report Country1b.FRX. As you remember, this is the report with the "improved" DataEnvironment handling you prepared earlier in the tutorial. You don't need to save this report to another report name, because you're not going to change the report this time; you just export the DataEnvironment information to a class library.

From the **File** menu, choose **Save As Class…**, invoking the dialog you see in Figure 46. This dialog has a number of disabled options right now (the disabled options are not used for reports). You must choose a name for your new class (I used **deCountry** in the sample) and you must also supply the name of the class library to hold the class (I used **WorldData** – the VCX extension is assumed if you don't add it). You can also add an optional description for the class. When you press **OK** in the dialog, VFP creates the class library.

> *The WorldData class library delivered with your samples includes the finished versions of all the classes for this tutorial, so if you work with this library directly the contents look somewhat different from the initial screen shots here, all of which show the library being created from scratch.*
>
> *While following these instructions, you can save your versions of the classes to a VCX with a different name to see results identical to the screen shots.*

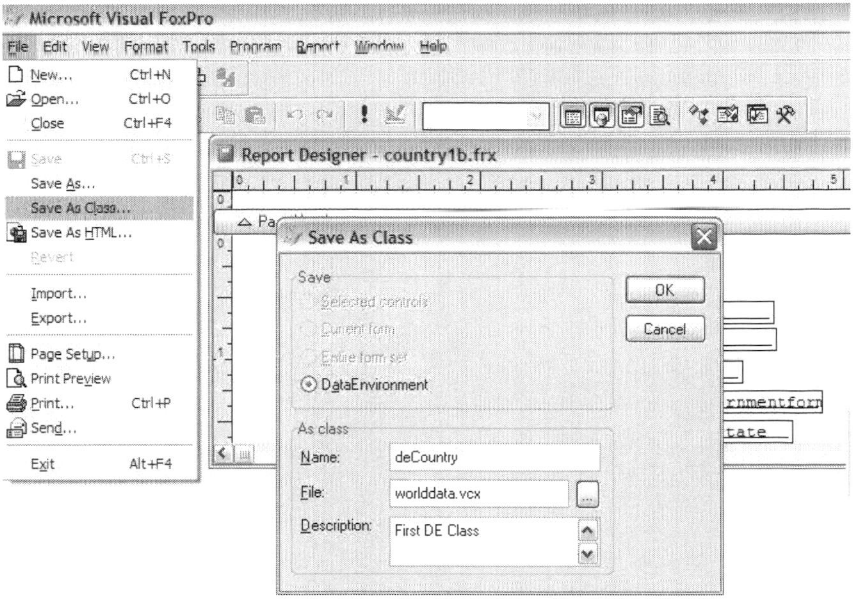

Figure 46. Exporting a DataEnvironment class definition from a report.

To see what you exported, you can open the new class in VFP's Class Designer. Although VFP offers several ways to open the class from the IDE, it is easy to find the class you created by typing the command **MODIFY CLASS ?** directly into the Command Window. A dialog allowing you to pick a class library (VCX). When you highlight the name of the class library in the left-hand list, you can then edit any class definition within the library. In your case, there is only one class in the library; the dialog looks something like Figure 47.

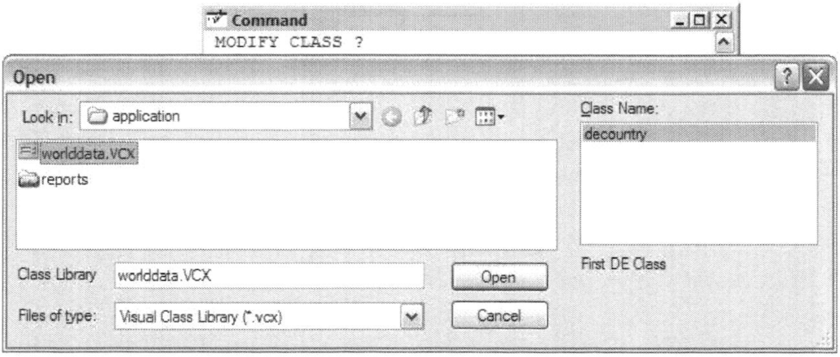

Figure 47. Opening a class in a Class library.

The new class looks significantly different from the contents of the Data Environment Designer you used earlier, as you can see in Figure 48. But, as you explore them in the Properties Window, you find that the attributes for the Data Environment parent object and its cursoradapter have been exported correctly.

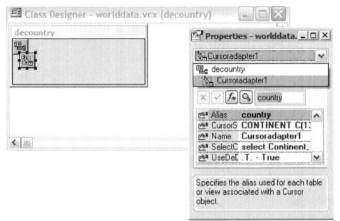

Figure 48. A Data Environment as a visual class, with a cursoradapter member.

Make a change to this class, by adding a field from the Country table that you didn't include earlier. (In the sample, I've edited the **SelectCmd** property to include the expression **UPPER(Name) AS UName** and added **UNAME C(44)** to the **CursorSchema**.) Then save the class and close the Class Designer.

6.2 Adding your VFP DataEnvironment class' data-intelligence to a report

Now you can use this class to give information to one or more reports. To test it, start with any of the Country*.FRX reports you created earlier (I used Country3.FRX). Save it to a new name (I used Country_With_Class). Use the **Report** menu's **Load Data Environment...** option again, but this time choose to **Link to a DataEnvironment class** before you press the **Select...** button in the Report Properties dialog. This time, you have access to the same dialog you used earlier to pick a class to modify in the Class Designer, rather than the standard File Open dialog, so you can pick your new class library and your new class.

You must confirm that you intend to replace the contents of the Data Environment for this report, as you did earlier. When you press **OK** in the Report

Properties dialog, and check the Data Environment Designer, you should see
the difference.

You can quickly verify that the field you added to the **CursorSchema** is
available in the new Data Environment, as I've done in Figure 51 below. But,
when you examine the attributes of the Data Environment and its cursoradapter more carefully, you notice that it isn't exactly the same as what you
saw in the Class Designer, which was a reasonable facsimile of the original
Data Environment attributes in the FRX from which the class was exported.

Some of your instructions, such as the **SelectCmd**, appear to be missing, and
there are quite a lot of methods with code in them with a heading similar to
what you see in Figure 49.

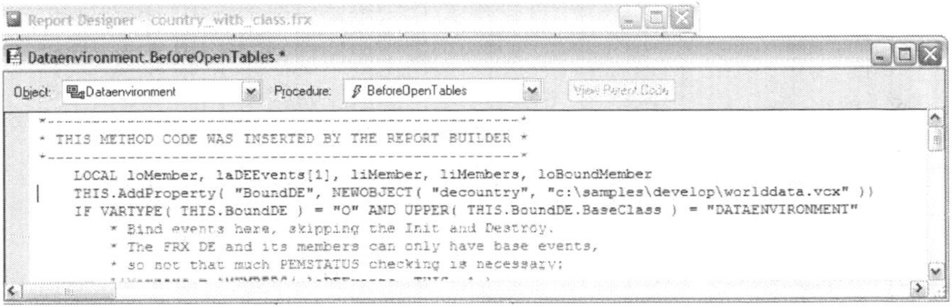

Figure 49. Report Builder- generated code in the Data Environment.

Don't be concerned. The Data Environment you see visually represented in
the Data Environment Designer is now just a placeholder for the design session. When you linked the report with a class, the Report Builder (which provides the Report Properties dialog for the Report Designer) wrote some additional code to instantiate your actual class, from the class library, to provide
your real instructions, when you run the report.

You also may notice that the Report Builder stores complete path information for your Data Environment class; you find this reference in the Before-
OpenTables generated code (shown in Figure 49).

> *If you have VFP 9 SP 1 or later, the Report Builder offers an option to omit
> this path information. In your sample code, I have removed the complete path
> information that the 9.0 original release Report Builder put in. The complete path
> information should not pose a problem at runtime in your applications, if you use the
> methods I recommend later in this tutorial. However, it may be an issue during de-
> velopment if you move your report around or rename a directory.*

You might have to re-locate the class library for the Report Builder when you
open my version of the Country_With_Class report, before you can preview
this report. Although I have removed the full paths from the Report Builder
code in this sample, the two files (class library and report form) are in two dif-

ferent directories. Without any path information, whether the report previews correctly depends on your current directory in Visual FoxPro when you modify the report.

> *VFP has mechanisms similar to PHP_CLASSPATH and Java's facilities for setting CLASSPATH and other search paths. For your design sessions, if you have set your current directory to the sample Reports directory, you can ensure the availability of the sample WorldData class library by using the following command:*

```
SET PATH to (GETDIR())
```

Choose the directory containing the VCX file from the dialog that appears (see Figure 50).

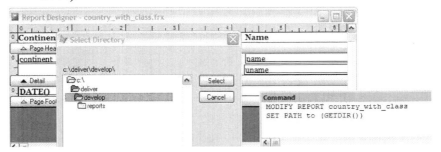

Figure 50. Adding the class library directory to your VFP search path for a design session.

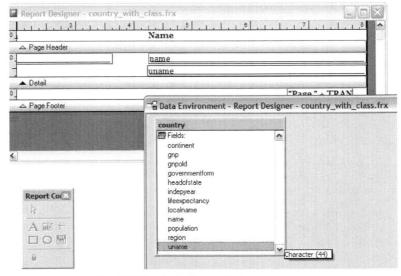

Figure 51. Designing with a DE Class in the Report Designer.

You can drag and drop the new column you added into your report layout, as I've done in Figure 51 above. When you save and run this report, you should see the additional content you specified, demonstrating that the report uses your class's SelectCmd attribute.

Now you can see how you can share one definition with multiple reports, and easily share any modifications you might make, such as changes in the definition of a calculated column, between multiple reports.

If you had a more complex Data Environment, such as the one required for the multi-detail-band World report you created earlier, with code setting up indexes and relations, you could create it in one report, test it, and then save it to a class library for repeated use. Your index-creating code is contained in the class and invoked for all the linked reports.

> *I've performed these steps and created a sample class, as* **deWorld**, *in the* **WorldData class library. I made a similar change to the Country columns, adding an uppercase version of the Name, and linked this class to a new report with the name* **World_With_Class.FRX** *(removing the Builder-generated full path information, as before). The new report uses the additional column value.*
>
> *Be careful not to link a class into a report, save the results back to a class library (where it will contain all the Report Builder's generated code), and then link your new class into reports, because the results could be recursive!*

This process -- rapid data design with quick tests of the result by previewing the report, and then saving the details of your design to a class library when you're satisfied with it, so you can link it to multiple reports -- certainly saves you some work.

But there are still some details that you are repeating over and over, such as the required setting of **UseDEDataSource** and **FetchSize**, for each cursoradapter, and the creation of the temporary index tags for each relation. These details have nothing to do with your data scenarios and you shouldn't be distracted by them every time you work out a new data scenario you may want to use for a new set of reports. In addition, each of these classes contains a SQLSTRINGCONNECT statement that holds sensitive information: your server, user, and password values.

It's time to abstract these details into a separate class level, with some custom behavior and attributes that make it easier to separate the data-specific details from the generic methodology.

6.3 Introducing a generic VFP Class Library for Reporting

Your sample materials for this tutorial include another VCX file along with the class library that you created: VFPREPORTS.VCX (in the "develop" folder). This class library provides superclasses with appropriate functionality, from which you can derive useful classes for working with the World database.

To examine the contents of this library, you could simply type **MODIFY CLASS ?** in the Command Window, or choose to **Open... Files of Type Class Library** (VCX) from the **File** menu. In the resulting dialog, if you highlight the VFPREPORTS library in the left-hand pane, you see the classes in this library, as shown in Figure 52.

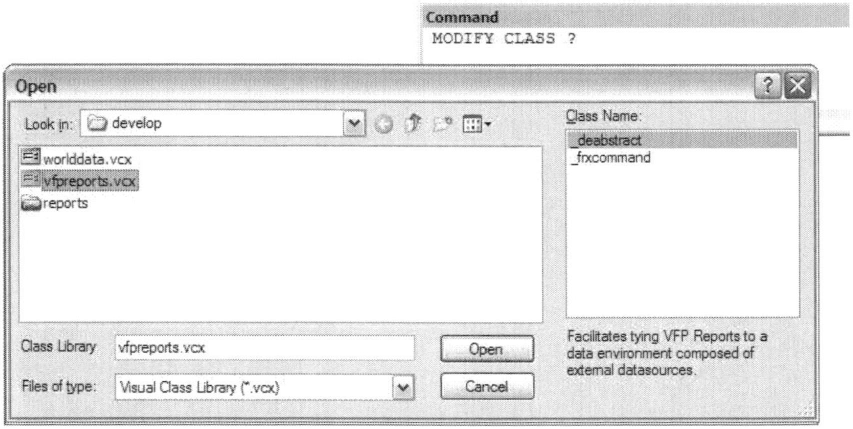

Figure 52. Choosing to open the VFPREPORTS class library.

However, to use this library, you don't need to open or modify its classes, so you can just click **Cancel** or press **Esc** if you are following along and have opened this dialog. Rather than choosing a class to open, explore the contents of this library using a different VFP tool: the Class Browser.

You find the Class Browser on the VFP **Tools** menu (see Figure 53). The **_deabstract** class currently highlighted on the left side adds some properties and methods (shown on the right side) to the DataEnvironment class.

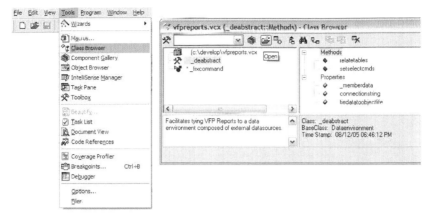

Figure 53. VFPREPORTS in the Class Browser.

For your next DataEnvironment class, derive from _deabstract rather than the DataEnvironment base class. You can do this directly in the Class Browser, by using a button four buttons to the right of the **Open** button. The correct button has a tooltip reading **New Class**; it is selected in Figure 54. When you click it, you invoke the dialog also shown in Figure 54. You can see that the ancestor class and its class library, VFPREPORTS.VCX, are already available. This dialog is also accessible using the **File** menu's **New...** option, or from the Command Window, as well as from the Class Browser, but you have to navigate to the correct class library and class name for the super class yourself.

Type a name for the new class; I used the class name NewWorld in the example.

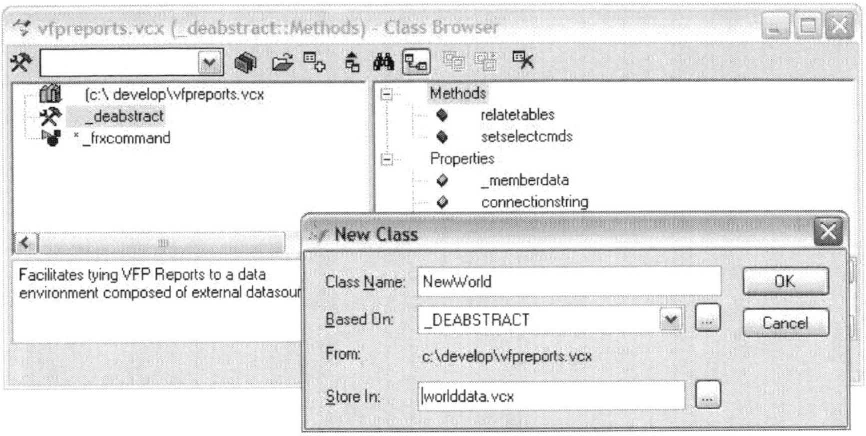

Figure 54. Deriving a class.

When you press **OK** in the dialog, the Class Designer opens, ready for you to add behavior to this class.

> *If you save the class at this point, you can tell the Class Browser to* **View** *MySQL* **Additional File**, *using the button with the "+" symbol immediately to the right of the* **Open** *button. When you've done this, you see the classes from both libraries on the left, with your new class represented in the inheritance tree. This view shows below, in Figure 57.*

The behavior you add to this class is only behavior that is specific to World data and its use in a particular report. For a first attempt, perform the following four actions:

Right-click on the surface of the class in the Class Designer and choose the **Builder** option from the context menu. A DataEnvironment Builder dialog appears (see Figure 55). Ignore all the items relevant to the DataEnvironment on the first tab, and switch to the second tab, where you can select **New...** to reach a nested, CursorAdapter Builder dialog. Change the Alias value in this dialog to something properly representing your data, such as **Country**, as shown in Figure 56, ignoring everything else in this dialog. When you press **OK** to exit the CursorAdapter Builder, press OK again to exit the DataEnvironment Builder too.

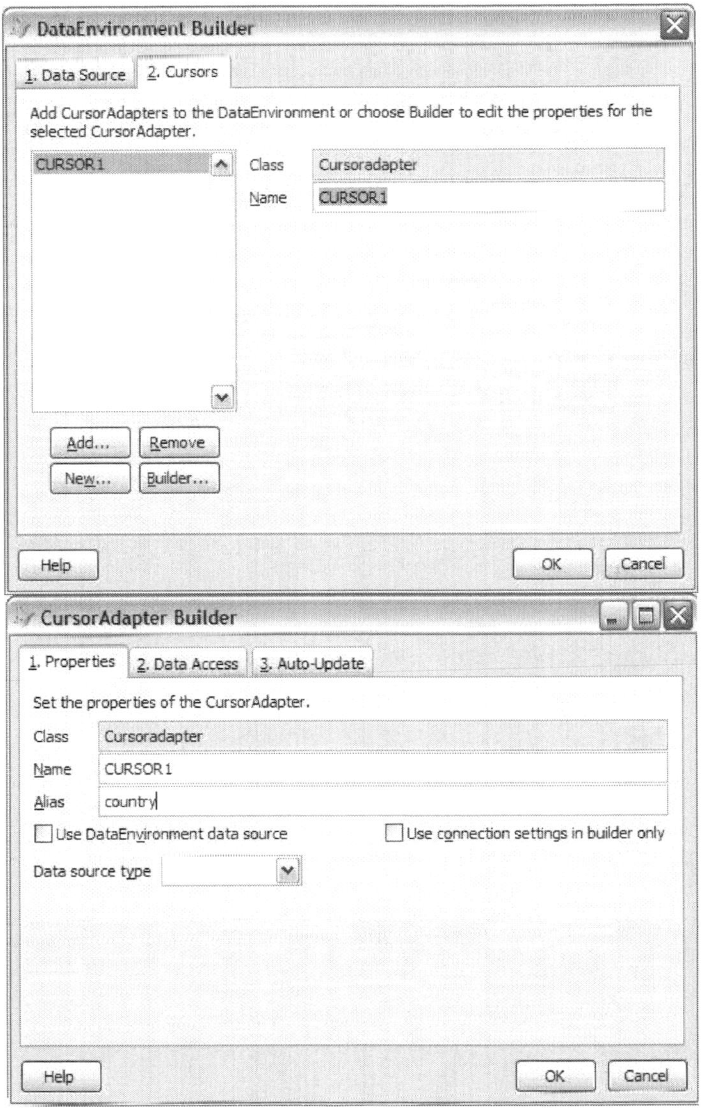

Figures 55 and 56. The CursorAdapter Builder and DataEnvironment Builder.

You now have a cursoradapter member contained in your DataEnvironment class, which you can verify by going to the Properties Window. Set the **SelectCmd** property, currently empty, to hold a reasonable SELECT statement, such as **SELECT Code, Capital, Continent, LocalName**

FROM Country. If you set the Properties Window to display **Non-Default Properties Only** you'll easily spot the one additional change to make: using procedures with which you are now familiar, set the **CursorSchema** to have a more useful value, such as **CODE C(3), CAPITAL I, CONTINENT C(13), LOCALNAME C(44)**.

With **Non-Default Properties Only** turned on, you may also spot some additional changes the Builders added to cursoradapter methods (probably to the AutoOpen and Init methods). If so, remove this code, which is unnecessary and not particularly useful.

Still in the Properties Window, turn your attention to the toplevel (DataEnvironment) object, setting its **InitiallySelectedAlias** property to the alias of your cursor (in the example, **Country**). Although setting this property value is not strictly necessary with only one cursor, it is a good habit. As a final required step, set the class's **connectionString** property, which you did not have in the base class DataEnvironment, to a string similar to the full value you used in the Command Window with the SQLSTRINGCONNECT() function earlier. For example:

```
DRIVER=MySQL ODBC 3.51
Driver;SERVER=localhost;DATABASE=world;USER=xx;PAS
SWORD=yy;OPTIONS=3;
```

You can save the class now; it's all ready to use in report design.

I've included a simple report, NewWorld1.FRX, that uses this class according to the technique established earlier in this tutorial:

I used the Load DataEnvironment function and selected my class.

When the Builder loaded my class into the Report's Data Environment, I dragged and dropped fields to the layout.

I removed the path information from the information the Report Builder added to my class (in the BeforeOpenTables method of the DataEnvironment).

When running my report, I made sure that the report and class library were in the same folder or, if they were not, I used the SET PATH statement described earlier to ensure availability of the class library.

What about the more complex functionality you added to your earlier reports, with multiple cursors and relationships? In your next class design experience, you'll add the minimal required information for the class to work out everything you need.

For this next trial, you could add some more cursors directly into this DataEnvironment class. But you might prefer to subclass from NewWorld, using the Class Browser, before adding more functionality. Which choice you make depends on whether you might ever use the simple class just the way it is, without additional overhead (the extra cursors and relationships).

In your samples, I've made the assumption that you might sometimes need only one cursor, so I've derived a new class from NewWorld, with the name NewWorldComplex. You can see its inheritance chain, using the Class Browser, in Figure 57. NewWorldComplex already has one cursoradapter object, inherited from NewWorld, so I've added two more cursoradapters to it, giving their **Alias** attributes the values **city** and **countrylanguage**, as you've done in each previous trial. I provided each cursor with appropriate values for its **CursorSchema** and **SelectCmd** attributes. To arrange the data more conveniently for grouping the data, I also edited the **SelectCmd** value for the country cursoradapter inherited from the ancestor class, this time including an **ORDER BY Continent, LocalName** clause. Because I did not need any additional columns in this cursor, however, I did not have to edit the **CursorSchema** value for the inherited cursor.

> *When I created each cursoradapter in the new class, I got rid of the pesky DataEnvironment Builder-written code in each cursoradapter object, by rightclicking to access* **Reset To Default** *in the Properties Window, as before. If you mistakenly open the CursorAdapter Builder for the inherited cursoradapter (with the alias* **Country**), *the Builder re-writes this code.*
>
> *Unlike the code the Report Builder writes in a report's Data Environment's method, the generated code written by the DataEnvironment and CursorAdapter Builders is not useful or required when you actually use these classes, whether in connection with reports or at any other time.*
>
> *It is always safe to remove this code, which is only useful for the DataEnvironment and CursorAdapter Builders' somewhat cluttered attempts to help the design process. You don't need their help, because you already have all the information you need to perform the (very simple) steps to design your cursoradapters and dataenvironments.*

In the Class Browser, you see the member objects added at each class level, so, with the NewWorldComplex class highlighted in Figure 57, you only see the two new cursoradapters in the right-hand pane.

Figure 57. Deriving a more complicated class.

All that's left is to set up the appropriate relationship code. As you remember, you wrote SET RELATION and INDEX statements earlier. This time, you add code to the getRelations method (inherited from the _deabstract class). Invoke the code snippet editor by double-clicking on the Class Designer surface, or doubleclick on any method attribute value in the Properties Window. Once you're in the code snippet editor, use the **Procedure** dropdown

at the top of the window to get to the getRelations method (see Figure 58).

```
* add two relations using the relation baseclass
* and set the desired relation properties:
IF TYPE("THIS.relation1") # "O"
    THIS.AddObject("relation1","relation")
    WITH THIS.Relation1
        .ChildAlias = "city"
        .ChildOrder = "CountryCode"
        .ParentAlias = "country"
        .RelationalExpr = "Code"
    ENDWITH
ENDIF
IF TYPE("THIS.relation2") # "O"
    THIS.AddObject("relation2","relation")
    WITH THIS.Relation2
        .ChildAlias = "CountryLanguage"
        .ChildOrder = "CountryCode"
        .ParentAlias = "country"
        .RelationalExpr = "Code"
    ENDWITH
ENDIF
```

Figure 58. GetRelation snippet for the NewWorldComplex class.

Here is the code for your NewWorldComplex class's getRelations method:

```
* add two relations using the relation baseclass
* and set the desired relation properties:
IF TYPE("THIS.relation1") # "O"
   THIS.AddObject("relation1","relation")
   WITH THIS.Relation1
      .ChildAlias = "city"
      .ChildOrder = "CountryCode"
      .ParentAlias = "country"
      .RelationalExpr = "Code"
   ENDWITH
ENDIF
IF TYPE("THIS.relation2") # "O"
   THIS.AddObject("relation2","relation")
   WITH THIS.Relation2
      .ChildAlias = "CountryLanguage"
      .ChildOrder = "CountryCode"
      .ParentAlias = "country"
      .RelationalExpr = "Code"
   ENDWITH
ENDIF
```

Although you may not be experienced at reading VFP code, you can probably see that this code is adding two new objects into the DataEnvironment container. As the comments at the top of the method indicate, these objects derive from the VFP relation baseclass. (You have already seen VFP in-line comments, which begin with "&&". In VFP, you can start a comment with "*" if it is on a line by itself rather than in line.)

Before the code creates each relation object, the TYPE() checks to see if the relation already exists because of some previous use of the object. The THIS keyword you see throughout the code references the DataEnvironment object in which the code is running, like $this in PHP, this in Java, and Me in VB. As in VB and Java, and similar to SQL's "table.column" syntax, you connect the THIS keyword with a "." character (you use "->" to do this in PHP). The AddObject function allows you to create a member object of a container object, such as the DataEnvironment.

Once each relation object exists in the container, the code changes four properties of the object, which indicate the cursors involved in the relationship and what columns in each cursor provides the relationship data.

> *Experienced VFP programmers may note that I have not used the .OneToMany attribute of each relation object in this code. Strictly speaking, if this class were to be used with forms, and if I wanted to indicate a one-to-many relationship, I would do so. As explained earlier in this tutorial, it is not necessary to do so for reports, since the Report Engine handles it for you.*

> *If you set this property explicitly, whether on some or all the relationship objects, the _deabstract class respects and uses it.*

This class is now ready to use with reports.

I've included a sample report using this class, NewWorld2.FRX. This report is not very different from previous trials you've done using multiple cursors (see Figure 59 for what it looks like), so I won't discuss its details except to note that it uses an IIF() ("immediate if") expression, to show which city for each country is the capital. Notice that you can include columns from multiple cursors in such an expression, in a Print When expression, or elsewhere in report output expressions. Just be careful to use the appropriate alias for the cursor owning each column in the expression.

> *If you are watching the report design and preview processing in the MySQL Administrator, or if you use the ASQLHANDLES() function in VFP, you may also notice one other aspect of reporting that has changed since you've started using the custom classes: the number of connections required to create these reports is much more tightly controlled.*

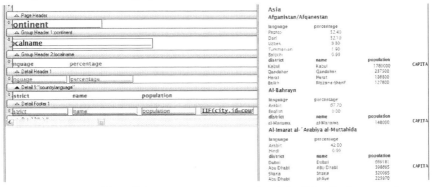

Figure 59. A report with multiple cursors uses your complex derived DataEnvironment class.

In the last example, you wrote code in the getRelations method that added two relation objects to the DataEnvironment and set their properties. In your next trial, you design two visual relation classes instead, using the Class Designer. You set their properties directly in the Properties Window instead of in code. You write slightly less code in the getRelations method to include instances of these two new visual classes, without needing to set their properties in code.

> *In this tutorial, the goal is for you to have to write as little code as possible to perform complex tasks, so I provide both methods.*

> *However, I honestly don't think there is that much difference between designing the visual relation classes and writing the relation code you wrote above.*

> *Some people like to design visual classes and others find the Properties Window takes more time to use than it takes to write the code to set the properties. Just try both, and use the design method that feels natural to you. There is little, if any, performance difference, and the resulting data should be the same -- so it is just a matter of taste.*

First, derive a new class from NewWorldComplex. As shown in Figure 60, I've called it NewWorldVisual.

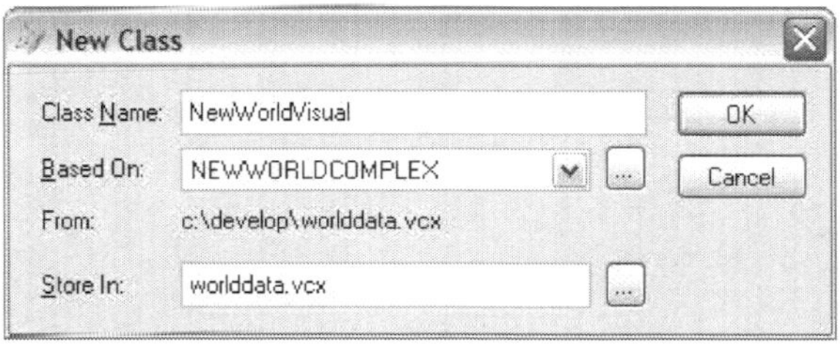

Figure 60. One more DataEnvironment class level.

Next, override the code you wrote last time, in the getRelations method. After you open the new class in the Class Designer, you can double-click on the surface of the Class Designer to bring up the code snippet editor. Navigate to the getRelations method using the **Procedure** dropdown, or from the Properties Window, as you've done previously.

> *When you navigate to the getRelations method, the method is initially blank, but you can refresh your memory of the NewWorldComplex code if you like; just press the* **View Parent Code** *button at the right in the snippet editor. You can see this button in Figure 61, and the parent class code shows below the new class's code.*

Here is the code snippet for this class' getRelations method. You haven't created the relation classes referenced in this snippet yet, but that's okay; you create them in the next step, before trying to test the class:

```
IF ATC(THIS.ClassLibrary, SET("CLASSLIB")) = 0
   SET CLASSLIB TO (THIS.ClassLibrary) ADDITIVE
ENDIF
IF TYPE("THIS.relation1") # "O"
   THIS.AddObject("relation1","relCountryLanguage")
ENDIF
IF TYPE("THIS.relation2") # "O"
   THIS.AddObject("relation2","relCountryCity")
ENDIF
```

This code ensures the availability of your two specialized Relation classes, since they will no longer be base class objects, using the SET CLASSLIB statement. It also checks to see if each relation member object already exists in the DataEnvironment container, as did the ancestor class code. If a relation object does not exist, the code creates an instance, using AddObject(), as before, but specifying your class name.

> *VFP programmers might wonder why we don't add the visual relations in a more "visual" way, perhaps by dragging instances of the derived classes we create from a customized toolbar or toolbox. If you do this, the relation objects are instantiated too early; _deabstract does not have an opportunity to create appropriate indexes for these external data sources.*

You notice that the SET CLASSLIB statement uses the expression **(THIS.ClassLibrary),** which indicates that you might expect these new classes to be found in the same class library as your DataEnvironment class (WORLDDATA.VCX in your samples). Your next task is to create these simple objects in the class library in which NewVisualWorld expects to find them.

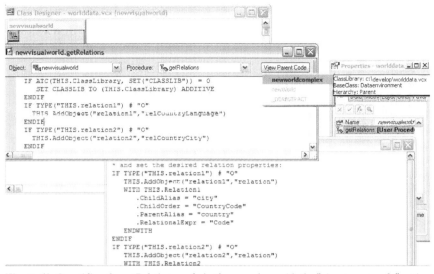

Figure 61. Overriding the getRelations code in the new class, with the "view parent code" option showing the parent-level version of the code behind this class's version of the method.

You can create your first Relation class directly from the Relation baseclass. You haven't done this before, because you started your first DataEnvironment class design process by saving a class from a report. However, creating a new Relation from scratch is extremely simple.

You can use the **New...** option on the **File** menu, the Class Browser's New Class button, or simply type **CREATE CLASS** in the Command Window. In the dialog, use the dropdown to pick the Relation baseclass for the **Based on** item; you'll notice that, when you do this to select a baseclass, you don't supply a class library for the **From** item. For the class name, I like to use something that suggested the relationship, going from parent to child; in this case, **relCountryCity**. Make sure to indicate that you want to save your class to your class library (here, WORLDDATA.VCX), as shown in Figure 62.

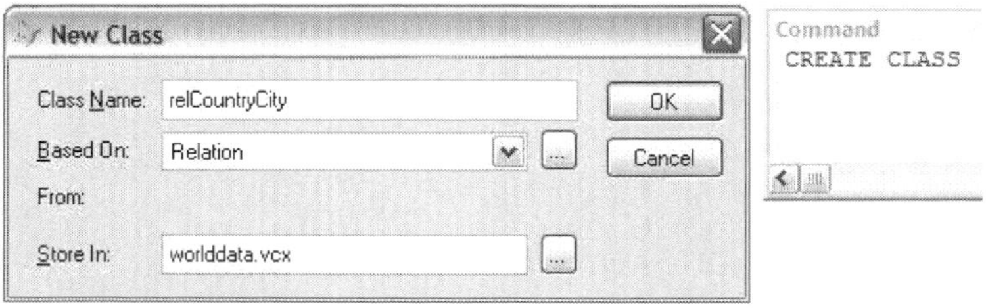

Figure 62. Creating a relation class from scratch.

In the Class Designer, you only need to change a few properties and, from writing the code previously, you probably already know what they are. (If you are not sure, you can check the Parent Code showing in Figure 61!)

- The **ChildAlias** is `city`.

- The **ChildOrder** is `CountryCode`.

- The **ParentAlias** is `country`.

- The **RelationalExpr** (the field on the parent side of the relationship) is `Code`.

With only non-default properties showing, your result should look like Figure 63.

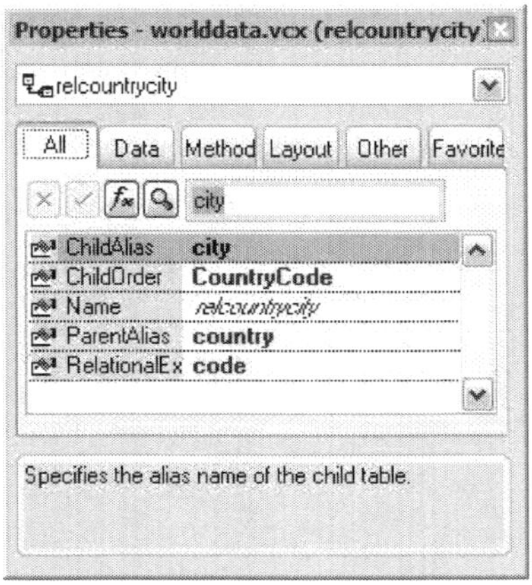

Figure 63. Relation attributes.

To create the second relation, you could do the same thing, but you don't really need to; the second relationship has the same ChildOrder, ParentAlias, and RelationalExpr values, but a different ChildAlias (`countrylanguage`). In this situation, you might decide to subclass relCountryCity to create the new relCountryLanguage class.

If you take this approach, as I have in your samples, and display both the VFPREPORTS and WORLDDATA class libraries in the Class Browser, your class hierarchy resembles the Class Browser window shown at the left in Figure 64. The figure also shows the Properties Window for the new relCountryLanguage class you created, on the right and the one property you changed in this class.

> If you change your mind about this class hierarchy decision later, you can "reinherit" or "redefine" the parent for a class using the Class Browser. You can also use the Class Browser to rename classes, as you refine your work. It's common to revise class hierarchies as you work on data schemas and scenarios.

Figure 64. Your class hierarchy complete with both Relation classes, and the one property you change to create the second derived Relation class.

Your NewVisualWorld DataEnvironment, which references these two visual relation classes, is now ready to work with reports. I created a report (NEWWORLD3.FRX) that uses this class for your samples by making a copy of NEWWORLD2.FRX and changing the one line of code in the Before-OpenTables method of the DataEnvironment that references the class used from NewWorldComplex to NewVisualWorld (see Figure 65). After making this change, the NEWWORLD3 report works exactly the same way as NEWWORLD2.

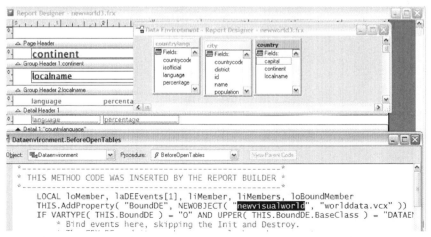

Figure 65. Using NewVisualWorld class in a report; simply change the name of the class.

6.4 Running the report with your DataEnvironment

The types of design and development work you've just done really showcase the strengths of object-oriented programming and object inheritance as applied in VFP. By changing a minimum number of elements, you can get the maximum value of re-use across different situations, both for your initial development work and to leverage any subsequent changes in your database. You can finely control the behavior of all your reports by controlling the behavior of a few ancestor classes.

But you can take this control even further. So far, you have had no control of how many times your database was accessed or exactly when the queries took place, because each report automatically accessed the database when you invoked the REPORT FORM command or previewed your results from the Report Designer. In fact, if you SET REPORTBEHAVIOR to 80 (backward compatible) and then to 90 (object assisted) you may even have noticed that the timing and number of database queries is different between the two modes.

To exercise more control, you need to change two properties of your DataEnvironment-derived class: AutoOpenTables and AutoCloseTables. I have created such a class, deriving it from NewWorldComplex. (It doesn't matter whether you derive this class from NewWorldComplex or NewVisualWorld.) As you can see in Figure 66, I've set both attribute values to **.F. - False**. Now you can explicitly open the tables, using the class's OpenTables method, whenever you're ready.

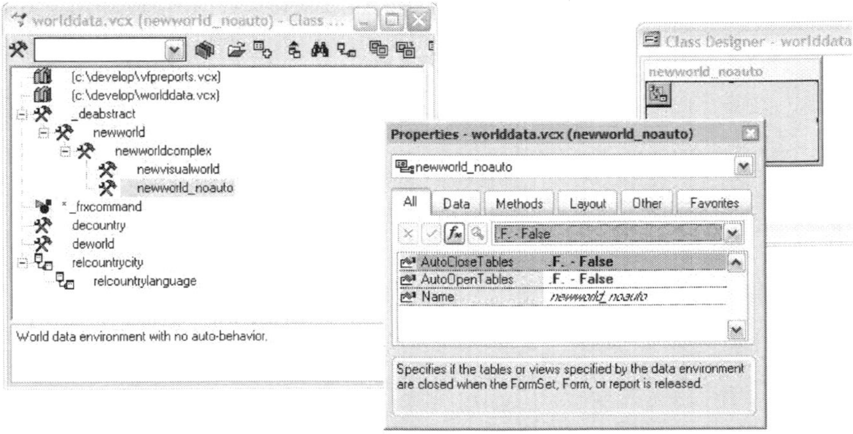

Figure 66. Turning off Automatic Behavior in a DataEnvironment-derived class.

To see how this might work, I've created a report, NEWWORLD4, which looks identical to other NewWorld-based reports in the Report Designer. However, the DataEnvironment is completely empty, except for a check I've added to its Init method, which stops the report run if there is no data available to run it (see Figure 67). If you try to preview the report, either from the Report Designer or from the Command Window, you see a messagebox indicating the problem, and no report appears (see Figure 68).

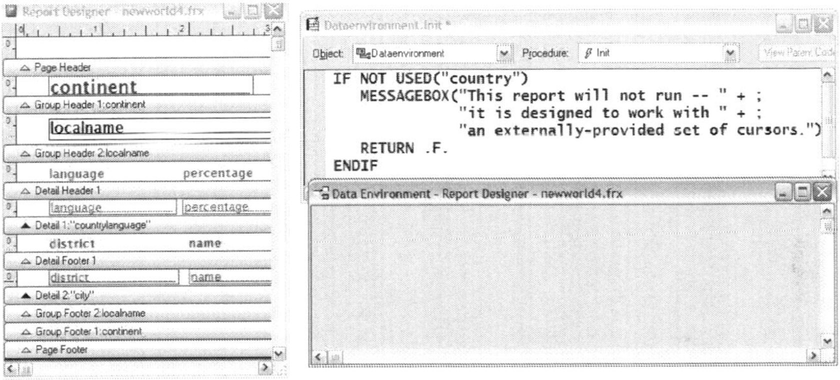

Figure 67. A report with an empty DataEnvironment...

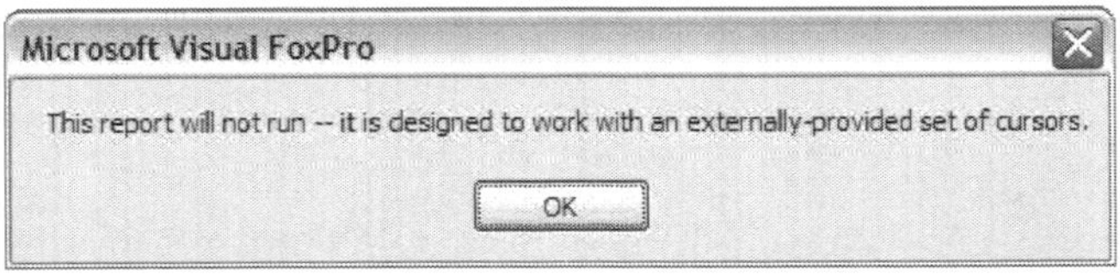

Figure 68. ... and the results if you attempt to run the report without providing data for it.

To run this report, you can create an instance of the class you just created, in the Command Window, using the syntax below, and then instruct the class to fetch the data. As discussed earlier, you need to use a SET CLASSLIB or SET PATH statement to make the class available unless you are in the directory containing the class library before you run these three lines of code:

```
MyObj = NEWOBJECT("NewWorld_NoAuto", "WorldData")
MyObj.OpenTables()
SET
```

The third statement opens the Data Session window (see Figure 69), so that you can verify your cursors are now open and available.

With this environment already set, you can run NewWorld4 (the report with no DataEnvironment instructions).

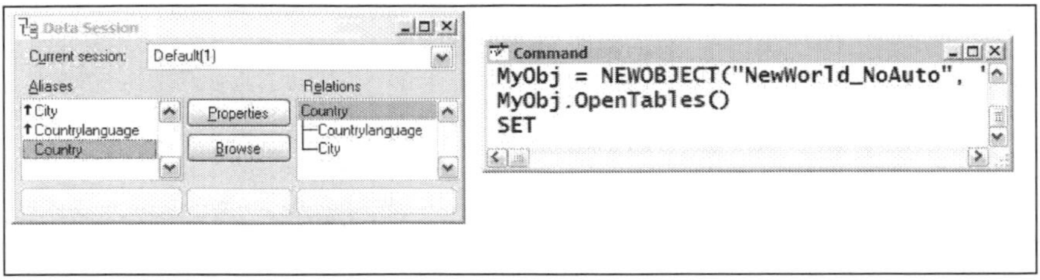

Figure 69. Explicitly opening tables using your class.

You could adjust all the other NewWorld* reports to use this technique as well, simply by changing the class referenced in their BeforeOpenTables to NewWorld_NoAuto, similar to what you see in Figure 65. (You could also Load the DataEnvironment using the Report Builder again, of course, and remove path information from the results.) This means you would have all the advantages of the cursors in the Data Environment Designer so you could drag and drop fields to the report design surface.

I've provided a report bound to the NewWorld_NoAuto class, with the file-name NEWWORLD5.FRX. This report also has its **AutoOpenTables** and **AutoCloseTables** attribute values set to **.F. - False**, similarly to the class.

When you are ready to preview your work from the Designer for NEWWORLD5 or any other report bound to this class, you can make the cursors available using two lines of code to instantiate your object and open the tables explicitly, as shown above. If you forget to do so, the report does not preview from the Designer; you receive an "Open" prompt from the Report Engine, which is trying to find an Xbase table on disk. Of course, you won't be able to use that dialog to access your cursor adapters, so the report doesn't run.

You can design many reports during the VFP session, using these cursors for design-previewing purposes. Because you have turned off the AutoClose behavior as well as AutoOpen, these cursors remain available until you RELEASE the MyObj variable or perform some other task in VFP that sends the object out of scope (for example, a CLEAR ALL command).

The data connection remains available along with the cursors. This means you can issue additional queries against your database, by filtering the data differently (as you'll see in the next section of this tutorial), or by re-using the data connection handle for multiple DataEnvironment objects, using code like the following:

```
SQLDISCONNECT(0) && disconnect all connections for
a clean test

* create and use one data connection to the World
database:
MyObj = NEWOBJECT("NewWorld_NoAuto", "WorldData")
MyObj.OpenTables()

* create a second object accessing World data with
different cursoradapters:
MyOtherObj = NEWOBJECT("SomeOtherWorld_DE_NoAuto",
"WorldData")

* give the second object a handle to the existing
connection
* and open tables as usual:
MyOtherObj.DataSource = MyObj.DataSource
MyOtherObj.OpenTables()

? ASQLHANDLES(xx) && shows you only one handle
```

> *Although you have turned off "automatic" closing behavior, you'll discover that the _deabstract class takes care of automatic cleanup, of both the cursors and the connection it has maintained to your database. Each instance of this class knows whether it has opened the connection itself, and destroys the connection when it goes out of scope.*
>
> *Therefore, when you execute* **RELEASE MyObj** *or* **CLEAR ALL** *after the test in the code above, you can issue* **? ASQLHANDLES(xx)** *again; the number of handles is 0.*

Also, because these cursors were externally opened and are in your working environment, the Report Builder shows you more information when you access the Expression Builder dialog while building an expression for any layout control (see Figure 70).

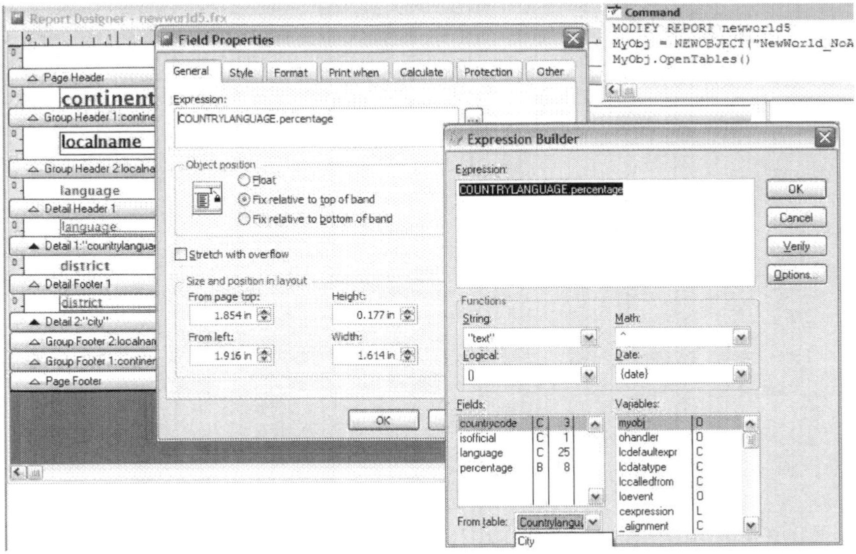

Figure 70. Data Availability in the Expression Builder when the Data Environment is independent of reports.

> *When working with multiple reports with one data environment, remember to turn off the AutoOpenTables and AutoCloseTables properties for the DataEnvironment in the report as well as your class, to be safe.*

If you've gotten yourself into the good habit of providing an InitiallySelectedAlias for each report, even when the report has only one cursor and it didn't seem necessary, you now find that is easier for different reports to share a single DataEnvironment definition. The InitiallySelectedAlias required for each report may not match the InitiallySelectedAlias of the DataEnvironment class.

You can add the following code to the OpenTables method of the report's DataEnvironment, assuming you've set the property for the report:

```
SELECT (THIS.InitiallySelectedAlias)

DODEFAULT() && perform any default chores
```

Alternatively, you can also SELECT the appropriate alias in code, between REPORT FORM statements. Methods presented in the next section of this tutorial make this easy to do.

Take a minute to think about other potential advantages to working with the already-opened cursors and manipulating your DataEnvironment class directly.

For one, if you set REPORTBEHAVIOR to 80, you won't see the data fetch as you move between pages in preview; both reporting modes are using already-prepared data in a consistent manner.

To illustrate a further advantage, issue the following line of code in the Command Window:

? MyObj.connectionString

You can see the results in Figure 71. The custom property connectionString, provided by _deabstract, is a readwrite value, which you can manipulate before issuing your OpenTables statement.

Figure 71. You can manipulate the connectionString property programmatically.

Rather than storing your sensitive database access directly in the property, as you've done in this tutorial so far, you can use the class to set the property dynamically in code, right before you run your report.

One obvious use of this capability is to test against different servers with different data sets and different user rights. But the feature also allows you to store the information elsewhere, in whatever secure fashion is appropriate to your application and only assemble the connection string within your code.

> *If you have explored the options on the Report menu, you may have noticed an item labeled* **Private Data Session**.
>
> *This option has nothing to do with security, although it might appear to, from its name. It is also not an appropriate option for the external datasource-centric report applications covered in this tutorial, because it's designed to shield data, and data settings (such as SET CENTURY) from one part of your application from use by another. In this tutorial, you concentrate on sharing data and data settings from one report result to another, for the greatest efficiency in database access.*

The _deabstract class provides a protected setConnectionString method, which you might implement by decrypting the values in a configuration file. The next section of this tutorial considers your options and approaches for this requirement further.

6.5 Moving on to a VFP reporting application

This section concludes your consideration of DataEnvironment-related class design techniques with external data for your reporting purposes. You now know how to assemble reports and how to attach your data to these reports, with efficient design techniques and runtime data-fetching techniques.

So far, you've run your reports in the Command Window or previewed them from the Report Designer. Now it's time to learn how to deploy them in a production environment after you've created and tested them.

In this section, you've learned to leverage the _deabstract class to provide appropriate behavior for your reports. In the next section, you leverage another custom class, and more VFP tools, to provide generic, flexible, and efficient report-running behavior.

You'll build your custom class library for data access into a VFP application along with the source materials supplied with this tutorial, and learn how to configure it to run whatever reports you create by supplying it with XML configuration files. You'll also be able to provide design sessions appropriate to your end-users, with the same application.

Chapter 7
Create a VFP reporting application

There are as many ways to create an application to deliver VFP reports as there are people who program in VFP. In this tutorial, my goal is not to teach you about all of them!

You have already learned to use VFP to create exciting and rich report layouts that leverage your data. Now you just want to get this layout in front of your users. My goal is to give you a simple set of steps that help you do it.

You will use some additional components I've supplied, along with the _deabstract class you have already used. You use these components to compile a generic executable (EXE) and a DLL. The EXE will allow command-line and ActiveX use of your reports, and the standalone DLL will allow some ActiveX use (without delivery of the EXE if you don't need it).

The EXE and DLL will include the VFPReports class library, your customized class library (such as WorldData), and some additional customizing instructions found in easily-edited text files.

You will deliver the EXE and/or the DLL, the supporting Reporting Application components and VFP runtime files, and your reports, to customer sites, using a standard SETUP.EXE I'll also show you how to build.

To set up your data and run reports, or to allow your customers to modify reports, you (or your external applications, such as PHP scripts on a web server) will create sets of XML instructions, describing any setup conditions and the reporting task or tasks to be performed. You will supply the EXE or ActiveX component with the XML instructions as a string or filename, and these VFP applications will run your tasks.

You can supply the XML as external files along with the VFP applications, and allow your users to run the actions simply by dragging and dropping these files on the executable, or on a script file, if you like. Because the XML is external to the applications, you will also find that it is easy to generate completely new sequences of reports, and to target different output devices, on-the-fly, according to your users' needs.

That's the plan. Let's get started.

7.1 Introducing the _frxcommand object

As is typical in VFP development, you need a complex, purpose-built object designed to do most of the work "behind the scenes". As you'd expect in object-oriented development, you don't need to investigate this class or understand how it works to use it.

The object in question is _frxcommand; you'll find it in the same VFPREPORTS.VCX class library as the _deabstract class you've been using. Its job is to understand the XML request format I'll describe shortly, and to parse the XML to run your reporting tasks.

Unlike _deabstract, _frxcommand is not an abstract class. You don't derive additional, data-knowledgeable classes from it or add code to it; you use it directly for any reports and all data scenarios.

If you open VFPREPORTS.VCX in the Class Browser and examine its exposed properties and methods (see Figure 72), you won't find very many.

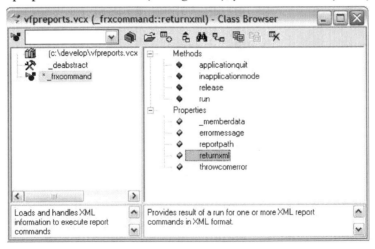

Figure 72. The _frxcommand object in the Class Browser shows few exposed properties and methods.

To use it, you need to know about even fewer properties and methods than you see in the figure. If you use it wrapped in an EXE file, you don't need to know about them at all. In this section, you build the EXE and ActiveX components for the first time, and use them immediately.

7.2 Building a VFP reporting solution

As delivered, your sample files include a "develop" directory with the files shown in Figure 73. Along with the generic VFPReports class library (VCX and VCT files), you see the fully-developed WorldData class library with all the data-customized classes created in earlier parts of this tutorial.

> *If you use the* **CD (GETDIR())** *command in the Command Window to navigate to the "develop" directory, you will save some time and confusion. If you don't do it, the build process you are about to run will still ensure that your current directory is this directory before it starts to work.*

When you create new reporting solutions based on this method, with different customized classes for different data sets, and different reports to go with them, you will create each solution in a separate directory. You can use the files you see here (except the WorldData class library) as a starter set of files, each time.

When you build a VFP Reporting Application for distribution, you want it to contain your custom classes for your data set. In the sample files for this tutorial this library is WorldData. For each application with different data, you'll probably use a different customized class library.

You customize each application's build process by adjusting some constants, including the name of your custom class library, in the file shown in Figure 73 as defines.prg. As you remember from looking at the UDF_GetDetails utility earlier, PRG is the default VFP extension for a program, or command file.

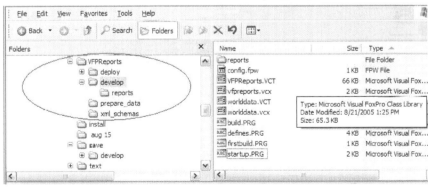

Figure 73. A Windows Explorer window shows sample folders for this tutorial, circled in red on the left, and the files initially available in the "develop" file folder, on the right.

You can open DEFINES.PRG file (remember, VFP and Windows don't care about preserving case!) for editing by choosing **Files of type Program** from the **File Open...** menu option. You can also type **MODIFY COMMAND ?** in the Command Window, as I have in Figure 74, below.

As you can see in the figure, this program file is basically a list of constants, an "Include" file for both programs and class library files.

If you are not familiar with VFP, you just need to know that VFP has a compile-time strategy for including files similar to PHP's **include <filename>** syntax and that of most other languages. The file extension does not have to be .PRG for these files, and most people prefer to use .H, for header file, as a convention.

> *If you are a VFP programmer and you wonder why I've used .PRG rather than .H in this instance, I've used DEFINES.PRG as the main program for the separate ActiveX-only project. I've also included EXTERNAL statements in this file, forcing external libraries to be pulled in during a compile. It also seems to force the Project Manager to "notice" any changes in the #DEFINEd constants during a recompile.*

DEFINES.PRG includes lots of features you can customize, such as all the text strings used by the application, which you will want to translate and personalize later. For now, just adjust the first two lines.

The first constant, MY_APP_NAME, which shows as "My Reporting Application" in the figure, is an easy way to "brand" various dialogs in the application, so change it to something that suits your needs.

The second constant, MY_APP_CLASSLIB, holds the name of your customized class library, so change it to whatever name you gave your library as you worked. You should not include the extension or the file path for this value.

When you have adjusted these two values, save this file using the same menu options or keystrokes you've used previously to save your work in a report design session. You are ready to build your application in two forms: an EXE and a DLL.

```
defines.prg *                                          Command
    * Include file for Generic VFP Reporting Application      MODIFY COMMAND ?
    * #DEFINEd constants for STARTUP.PRG
    * and the VFPReports.VCX Class Library.
    * >L< (c) Lisa Slater Nicholls 2005

    * ----- below are constants for you to tune for different applic

    #DEFINE MY_APP_NAME          "My Reporting Application"
    #DEFINE MY_APP_CLASSLIB      "WorldData"  && do not include VCX

    * ----- below are constants for you to tune for your general use
    * ----- which you can set but ordinarily will not need to change

    #DEFINE APP_MSGBOX_TIMEOUT   5000
    #DEFINE DEBUGGING            .F.
    #DEFINE USE_VFP9_REPORT_ENGINE .T.
    #DEFINE VFPREPORTS_CLASSLIB  "VFPReports"
    #DEFINE REPORTLISTENER_CLASSLIB "_reportlistener"

    * ----- below are strings you can adjust for languages, etc

    #DEFINE GENERAL_FAILURE_LOC  MY_APP_NAME + " failure: "
    #DEFINE MISSING_PARAM_LOC    MY_APP_NAME + ;
                                 " requires parameter to run: confic
    #DEFINE XML_ERROR_LOC        "XML load failure: "
```

Figure 74. Customizing your VFP Application's constants

I've included two "make" files, or build scripts, to help you build the application: FIRSTBUILD.PRG and BUILD.PRG. You can see them in Figure 73 above. The FIRSTBUILD.PRG creates VFP project files in support of the build process, the first time you use the process for any application, so you'll use that one now.

Run FIRSTBUILD.PRG by choosing the **Program Do...** menu option, or simply by typing **DO ?** in the Command Window and selecting the FIRSTBUILD.PRG file. If you have already used the CD command to navigate to the "develop" folder, you can also type DO FIRSTBUILD in the Command Window.

When you execute the FIRSTBUILD program, you see VFP start the build process. As it identifies dependent files required by your application, it asks you to Locate any files it can't find by itself. For example, the UDF_GetDetails.PRG file is in the Reports directory, and I have included a reference to this program in DEFINES.PRG. VFP may also ask you to find the library you referenced in MY_APP_CLASSLIB, if it is not in the "develop" directory.

Press the **Locate** button in the dialogs that come up during the build process (see Figure 75), and find these files for VFP. You will have to do so twice for each of these files, because you are building two separate projects.

When FIRSTBUILD.PRG finishes running, it opens both projects for you (see Figure 76).

Figure 75. Locate any dependent files for VFP during FIRSTBUILD.PRG's processing.

> *You may not need UDF_GetDetails.PRG to be built into every application if you're not creating the kind of reports that use this UDF. However, I've included it to illustrate the principle of Locating files and also because, once you have this tiny UDF bound into your application, you can add reports that reference it later, without changing your application at all.*

If you are absolutely sure you don't want this UDF and don't want to be bothered Locating it for the Project Manager, you can remove this line from DEFINES.PRG, or make it a comment by preceding the line with an asterisk:

* EXTERNAL PROCEDURE UDF_Getdetails.prg

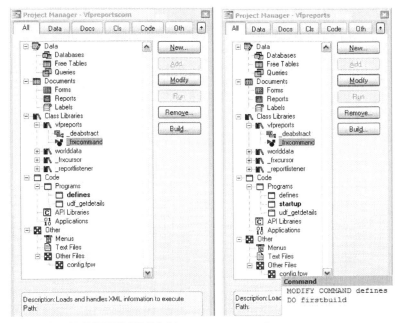

Figure 76. After FIRSTBUILD.PRG finishes, you see two projects.

If you expand the contents of the file trees in each project, as you see in Figure 76, you'll find that they are very similar. Neither have any Data or Document components.

You may be surprised that there are no reports in the projects, and wonder why I don't suggest you build all the reports you need into your applications. You can build the reports in (they will appear in the Documents section of the project tree), and many VFP programmers do.

However, I recommend you deliver reports separately on disk. This way, you and your users can edit them as needed, and you can add directly to the set of available reporting results, without making any changes to the application.

> *In a later section of this tutorial, you'll learn how to customize your end-users' design experience, should you choose to offer them this ability. You'll also learn how to configure the actual location of the reports on disk in your distributed application.*

Both projects have the VFPREPORTS class library plus the one that you indicated in the MY_APP_CLASSLIB constant (WorldData, in the figure). They both also have two other class libraries pulled in from the VFP installation files' FFC (Foxpro Foundation Class) directory, used by the _frxcommand class.

Each project also has a file of "Other" type, CONFIG.FPW, which is a special text file VFP uses to set up the environment. You'll learn about customizing this file later.

There is, in fact, only one difference between the two projects: VFPReports, which you see on the right side in Figure 76, includes a STARTUP code file, which is a stub program to invoke the _frxcommand class. VFReports is the project you'll use to build the executable (EXE), which includes both a command-line and ActiveX interface. VFPReportsCOM (on the left side in the figure) supports only the ActiveX component, and allows you to call the _frxcommand class directly from any external application supporting COM interfaces, so it doesn't need the STARTUP.PRG code.

When you check the "develop" directory, you find that the build process added quite a few files to the folder (see Figure 77). The PJX/PJT files are your new project files. You also see the new VFPREPORTS.EXE and VFPREPORTSCOM.DLL files, the final results of the build process you ran.

You can double-click to test the VFPREPORT.EXE file, or execute it from the command line; you should see the change you made to the MY_APP_NAME constant. In the figure, I edited DEFINES.PRG to use **ABC Corporation** for the value of MY_APP_NAME before I built the project and the EXE.

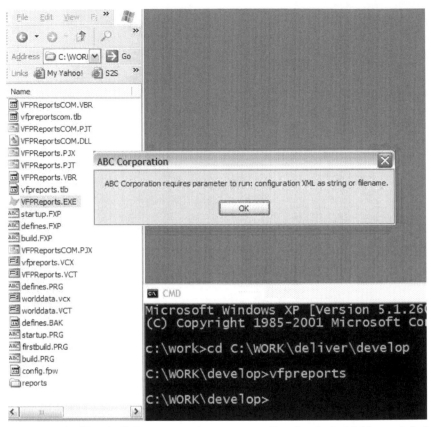

Figure 77. The "Develop" directory contains many more files after the build. The newly-built applications contain the changes you made.

Now that you have created your projects, you will not have to Locate the files for VFP again for this application. If you make any changes to DEFINES.PRG or your class library, you can rebuild the EXE and DLL with your changes using BUILD.PRG instead of FIRSTBUILD.PRG.

Now that the project exists, you can handle later builds differently. You can open either project file in the Project Manager tool, and use its **Build** option (available from the **Project** menu, shown in Figure 78, or within the Project dialog) to handle the build process. However, I find it handy to keep the projects in synch by using the BUILD.PRG script to build both at once.

> *The Build Options dialog you see in Figure 78 has an option to* **Recompile**
> **All Files**, *which is very useful if you're not sure VFP will see all your changes in dependent files.*

You can achieve the same thing by passing a parameter indicating "full recompile" to BUILD.PRG. You can use a Boolean .T., the numeric value 1, or the case-insensitive strings "yes", "on", or "true"; for example

DO BUILD WITH "YES"

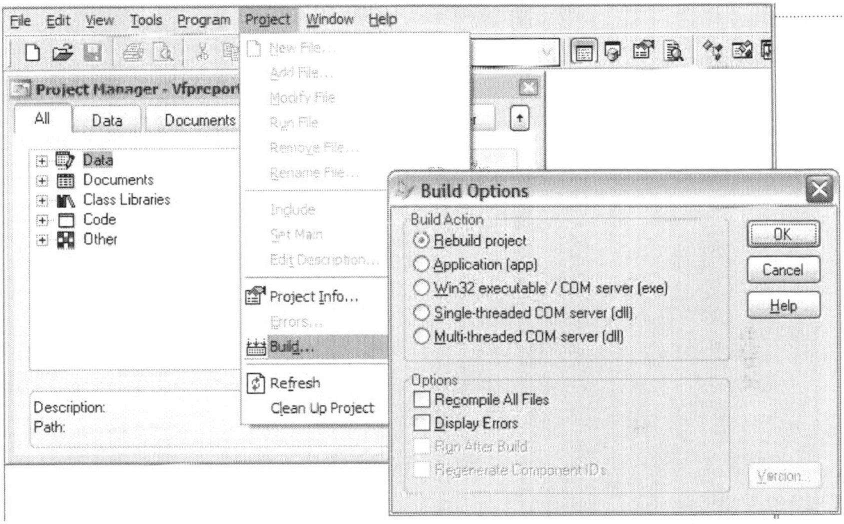

Figure 78. Rebuilding an application from the project.

7.3 Deploying your VFP reporting application

The "develop" directory includes the files you need to create and build your application. The "reports" directory (supplied as a subfolder of "develop", in your sample files) holds the reports for the application, which you develop and distribute along with the application.

To illustrate how the application functions when you distribute it, I've included a "deploy" directory in your sample files (see Figure 79). This folder includes some test scripts in batch (BAT) and VB Script (VBS) formats, as well as a selection of XML command files in the format understood by the _frxcommand object that drives your application. You'll use these XML files to try your first simple tests, before we delve into the structure of the command files themselves.

In the figure, you see a shared subfolder also named "reports"; I've included copies of three reports you've already developed in this folder. I've marked the subfolder shared in my copy, to illustrate that these reports might be in another network location in your real application.

Folders	×	Name	Size	Type
⊟ 🗁 deploy	▲	📄 testHtml.xml	1 KB	XML Document
🗁 reports		📄 testPrintPromptParameters.xml	1 KB	XML Document
⊞ 🗁 develop		📄 testModify.XML	1 KB	XML Document
🗁 prepare_data		📄 test.bat	1 KB	MS-DOS Batch File
🗁 xml_schemas		📄 testPreview.xml	1 KB	XML Document
🗁 install		📄 testCreate.XML	1 KB	XML Document
🗁 aug 15		📄 test.vbs	1 KB	VBScript Script File
⊞ 🗁 save		🗁 reports		File Folder
⊞ 🗁 text		📄 testNoFind.xml	1 KB	XML Document
⊞ 🗁 various resources		📄 testNotXML.xml	1 KB	XML Document
⊞ 🗁 working	▼			

Figure 79. The test deploy directory; copy your VFPREPORTS.EXE file to this location.

When I copied reports to the deployment folder, I chose these three reports, which are relatively complex and illustrate three different Data Environment strategies:

* -- UNRELATED_WORLD.FRX (which has no bound class);

* -- WORLD_WITH_CLASS.FRX (which uses an automatic connection strategy, using AutoOpen and AutoClose); and * -- NEWWORLD5.FRX (which requires the DataEnvironment object instance to be created before the report).

I wanted you to see that all three strategies will work.

However, in your application, I don't recommend you mix these tactics. As you probably realize, for production use, I think it is best to manage the connections and DataEnvironment objects externally, as you did in NEWWORLD5.FRX.

You also remember that NEWWORLD5 is the report that uses the external PRG (UDF_GetDetails.PRG), but the deploy\reports subdirectory does not include this file. Along with your class libraries, the PRG is now built into the EXE and DLL, so you don't need to distribute it.

To begin testing your application, copy the VFPREPORTS.EXE you've built into the "deploy" location. Don't worry about copying the DLL, because you don't need to move it to use the ActiveX objects while testing on your development machine.

You can test the EXE by dragging and dropping an XML command file on the EXE file, or by issuing the command **VFPREPORTS** followed by the name of the XML command file at a DOS prompt. You can also issue the **VFPREPORTS** command followed by the XML as a string, such as:

VFPREPORTS "<root/>"

If you use the string syntax or if your filename has spaces in it, you must enclose the argument in quotation marks, as shown in this example, to ensure that the operating system's command processor interprets the argument correctly.

Try accessing VFPREPORTS at a DOS prompt now, but use an argument that is not well-formed XML on the command line. You should see a message similar to Figure 80. If you drag the document named testNoXML.xml onto the EXE, you should see the same result, with a slightly different XML error reported.

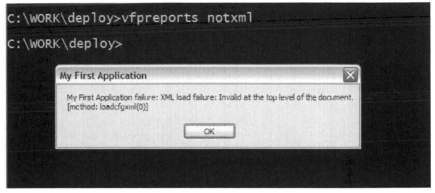

Figure 80. Passing VFPREPORTS ill-formed XML.

If, instead, you use the command shown earlier, **VFPREPORTS "<root/>"**, or any other well-formed XML, nothing will appear to happen. You will not be able to tell whether you processed reports or not. For example, try dropping the testNoFind.XML file onto the EXE. (This file includes the name of a report to process, but the report does not exist.) This is expected behavior for your VFPREPORTS application when no global error has occurred.

How will you know what occurred, and whether reports have been processed successfully or not? Just as _frxcommand accepts instructions as an XML file, it provides full results in the form of an XML document.

It's easiest to access the result data when you use _frxcommand as an ActiveX object, because the result document is exposed as a property of the object: returnXML. Using the ActiveX object from an external application requires the following simple steps:

1. Instantiate the object as appropriate for your development language, such as **$obj = new COM("<server>._FRXCommand")** in PHP. Because the _frxcommand object is available both from VFPREPORTS.EXE and VFPREPORTSCOM.DLL, this may be either VFPReports._FRXCommand or VFPReportsCOM_FRXCommand (see example script below).

2. Call the object's Run method, using either an XML string or the name of an XML command file to process as the method's argument, just as you did earlier on the command line.

3. Examine the results by using the object's returnXML member property.

I've written a short VBS script (TEST.VBS) and included it in the "deploy" directory. You can use this script by dragging an XML file to it, or from the DOS command line, similar to the way you use VFPREPORTS.EXE:

CSCRIPT TEST.VBS <filename>

Figure 81 shows you the way the results look if you use the command above with testNoFind.XML as its argument, and Figure 82 shows you the results of dragging and dropping this command file directly on the TEST.VBS script.

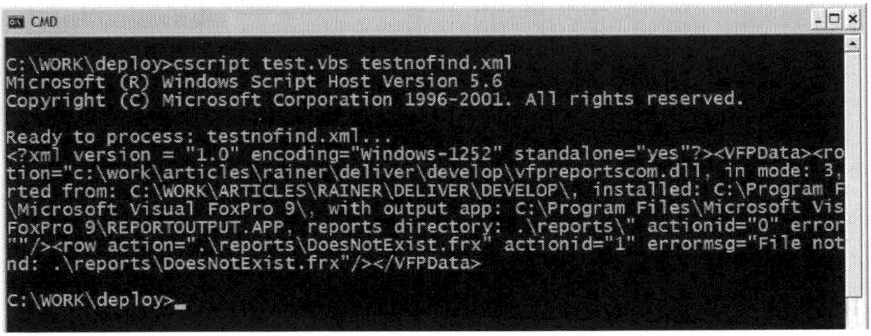

Figure 81. Calling _frxcommand as an ActiveX object from the command line....

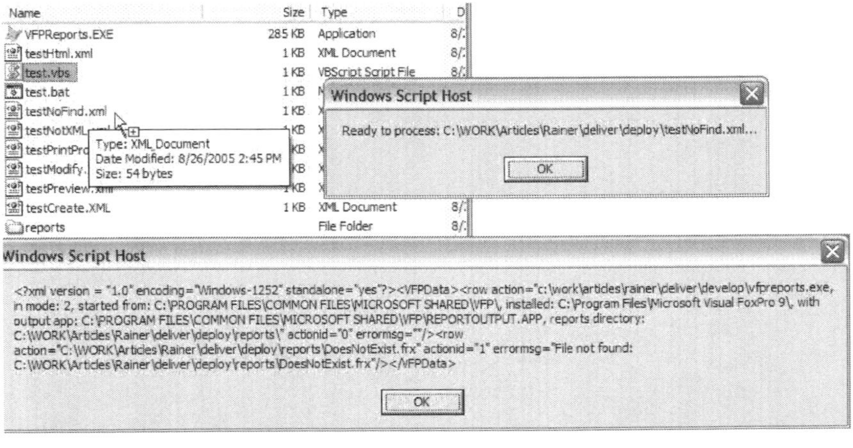

Figure 82. ... or using drag-drop.

When you examine the returnXML document, you see that it provides global result information and specific results for each report you want to process, and is easily parsed by any XML-handling mechanism available in your favorite development language.

Here are the contents of the TEST.VBS script file:

```
SET args = WScript.Arguments
IF  args.Count > 0 Then


  WScript.Echo "Ready to process: " & args.Item(0) & "..."


  IF Instr(args.Item(0),"\") > 0 Then
    ' drag and drop provides full path in the argument
    SET ox = CreateObject("VFPReports._FRXCommand")
    ox.Run(args.Item(0))
  ElseIf True Then ' EXE version will need full path
information
    SET ox = CreateObject("VFPReports._FRXCommand")
    SET ofs = CreateObject("Scripting.FileSystemObject")
    ox.Run(ofs.getFolder(".") & "\" & args.Item(0))
  Else
    SET ox = CreateObject("VFPReportsCOM._FRXCommand")
    ox.Run(".\" & args.Item(0))
  End If


  WScript.Echo ox.ReturnXML
End If
```

As you see, if you call the script with a filename argument, rather than using drag-drop, you must provide slightly more information (full path) when you use the version of _frxcommand bound into the EXE and exposed as an ActiveX control than when you use the DLL version. (You can easily provide the full path in both cases.) Note that the path for your command file may be UNC in style (\\server\path\filename). However, this version of _frxcommand does not accept URLs.

If the DLL version is more capable, why would you use the version of the ActiveX component provided in VFPREPORTS.EXE? For one small reason, the EXE includes both the command line interface and the ActiveX component in one file. More significantly, the EXE-based ActiveX control is better suited to handling reporting scenarios requiring user feedback, such as previewing reports or report design sessions. The DLL version of the ActiveX is most useful for server-based applications that generated printed reports, or report files.

Suppose you're using the VFPREPORTS application through the command-line interface, but still need to evaluate the success or failure of your report runs? _Frxcommand has a special method (logFeedback) designed to provide this behavior if you would like to add it (either in _frxcommand itself or a derived class). For example, you could log results to a text file, or save the results of each run to a database. As an alternative, you could also adjust STARTUP.PRG to do the same thing. You'll find that STARTUP.PRG is just a VFP version of the VBS script, instantiating the _frxcommand class and calling its Run method. Because STARTUP.PRG has a reference to the instance of _frxcommand, it can parse, and store or display, the contents of the object's returnXML property.

> The DEFINES.PRG file you adjusted earlier also has a DEBUGGING constant. You can set the value of DEBUGGING to .T. (True) if you want more feedback while developing an application but don't need this feedback in production runs. When this constant is set, you receive the full response XML in a message box, similar to the global error feedback you saw in Figure 80.

7.4 Understanding and preparing XML command files for _frxcommand

Now that you've run a few simple tests, you need to know how to give your VFPREPORTS application more complicated reporting instructions. As you know, you express these instructions as XML documents. For _frxcommand to parse your XML documents successfully, they must be valid according to _frxcommand's request schema.

You will find the full details of this schema in the file REQUESTXML.XSD, in the "xml_schemas" folder of your sample files. The XML documents in your "deploy" directory are all valid instances of this schema, highlighting different reporting scenarios. REQUESTXML.XSD contains documentation as well as the schema specifications. You can read the XML directly in an XML-capable browser or in your favorite XML editor.

If you are not used to reading an XML schema, you may find it difficult to understand the structure of the request document at first. Refer to the diagrams in this section to get a general idea of how to build the document, and then return to the XSD file for specific annotations and validation rules governing individual elements in the structure.

> The "xml_schemas" folder also contains RETURNXML.XSD, the schema for the returnXML document, which is much simpler (see Figure 83, which shows the schema with all its annotations).

Figure 83. The simple schema for the returnXML document.

In the request document structure, attributes on the root node specify global behavior for the full run (see Figure 84 – refer to the schema document for associated annotations). For example, the ReportPath attribute allows you to specify the directory on the server or on the network holding your report files. You can specify this value in UNC format and set it to a shared location: **ReportPath="\\servername\reports"**.

The value of the TopForm attribute indicates whether you want to use the VFP main form (Screen) or a custom VFP form to contain any visual elements, such as report preview and progress bar windows. Note: in this version, Report Designer sessions are forced to Screen even when you use this attribute on the root element. This limitation may be lifted in a future version.

The QuietMode attribute specifies whether you want to suppress user feedback throughout the run, and the PrinterName specifies the name of a Windows printer setup you want to use.

> *TopForm and **QuietMode** are both schema instances of a type declared in the schema as **FRXBooleanTrue**. When you investigate the schema type definitions, you find the FRXBooleanTrue type is restricted by a pattern declaring its allowable values, useful for validation purposes. You also find the following annotation to the type, which discusses the allowable values: The values 1, YES, TRUE, ON, or .T. (all case-insensitive) result in a VFP evaluation of Boolean-True. Anything else results in a VFP evaluate of Boolean False.*
>
> *I have included useful XML request examples in your "deploy" directory, and the elements I used in each example are discussed fully in this section. These examples give you sufficient syntax to handle many ordinary reporting scenarios. However, to fully appreciate the abilities of frxcommand in handling complex reporting command syntax, you must refer to the schema document.*

The DataEnvironment-related group of attributes are shown in a separate box in the diagram in Figure 84 because these attributes are defined together to form one schema type. DEClass and DEClassLib specify the name of a class and class library you want to open, to prepare your data before processing any reports. This group of attributes also includes DEConnectionString, for specifying the ConnectionString at runtime, and DEOpenTables, for indicating whether you want _frxCommand to open the tables for you explicitly before running the reports. The DEConnectionString and DEOpenTables attributes are optional in the schema type.

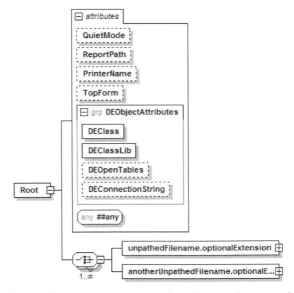

Figure 84. Specify global behavior by using root node attributes in the request document.

Within the root node, you place one or more elements indicating the name of report or label files you wish to run, or to open in a design session. These nodes are processed in the same order they appear within the root node of your document.

For each report row or action, use the actual name of the report or label (with no path) to name the report or label. In other words, where you see the word unpathedFilename.optionalExtension in Figure 84, substitute actual filename.

You specify attributes and child nodes for each report action node as appropriate for the individual report action you want to take. Some specifications have no meaning for a report design session and others are only valid for design sessions.

For each reporting action node, _frxcommand first evaluates attributes for the individual report elements (shown in Figure 85) to determine the report action type and its most significant behavior.

For example, the design attribute indicates whether you want to run the report or label, or to open a design session. If the design attribute is not present, the row processes a REPORT FORM or LABEL FORM command. If the attribute is present, the values 1, NEW, or CREATE (case-insensitive) result in CREATE LABEL or REPORT commands. Anything else results in a MODIFY REPORT or MODIFY LABEL command.

The fileType report action attribute indicates whether you wish to process the row using REPORT or LABEL syntax. The values 1 or LABEL (case-insensitive) for the fileType attribute result in LABEL FORM, or MODIFY or CREATE LABEL, commands. Anything else results in a REPORT command of the appropriate form.

The dialog attribute indicates that you would like an "open" dialog to appear if the report or label you have specified is not available.

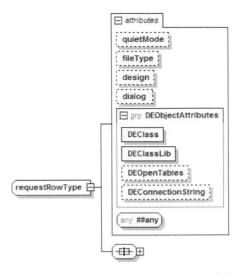

Figure 85. Specify a report or label to process by using an unpathed element name. To specify report-row behavior, start with a report row's attributes.

After _frxcommand evaluates the report element's critical attributes, it proceeds to evaluate the child nodes for the report row (see Figure 86). Most of the child nodes are analogous to clauses of the REPORT FORM and MODIFY REPORT commands. The child nodes for a reporting action can be complicated, because the REPORT FORM and MODIFY REPORT commands are themselves rather complicated.

For example, the objectType child node expresses the OBJECT TYPE <N> clause of the REPORT FORM and LABEL FORM commands. Its type attribute provides the numeric value associated with this clause, and its filename attribute provides the target filename for output generated as a file by this type, such as an XML or HTML file. You also find a file attribute directly on the request row, but this attribute is reserved for output generated by the VFP engine (typically, a printer file).

Notice the selectAlias node available on a request-row level. This element is particularly helpful when you have a DataEnvironment containing several cursors and you wish to specify a different driving alias for each report.

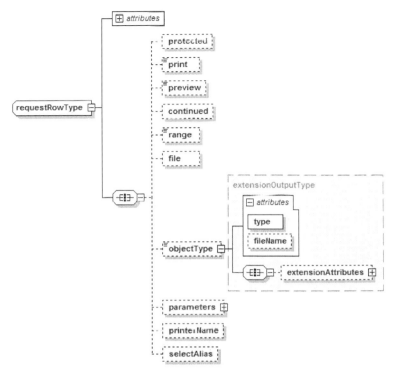

Figure 86. The child nodes express clauses of a reporting command.

Where settings are held on both global and row-level, the run uses your initial global settings until they are countermanded by a row-level setting. For example, you can set PrinterName at the beginning of a run, and then change printers using the printerName element of a particular request row.

Some settings repeated on both levels have slightly different behavior on the global and row-level. For example, if you set PrinterName on a global level to a printer setup that does not exist, this is considered a global error and the run does not complete. If, however, you set a printerName attribute on the row-level and the printer setup you name does not exist, the error is trapped, and reported in the result for the row, but the printer is set to the current default. The report processing continues with this information.

Differences of this sort are documented in the schema file, as illustrated in the diagram you see in Figure 87.

It is important to realize that a new setting on a row-level will have an effect on subsequent rows to which this setting may apply. If you want to revert to your original PrinterName value after setting printerName for one report, use the original value again for the subsequent report in the document. If you specify a Data Environment for one report and its tables are incompatible with the requirements of the next report, you must specify the Data Environment –related attributes on the subsequent report.

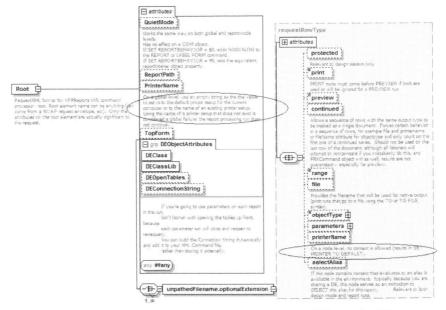

Figure 87. The request schema includes annotations on usage, which may be different on a global- and row- level for similar request value types.

When you examine the schema, you notice that the request row includes a parameters child node; this particular element does not correspond to anything you'll find in a REPORT FORM or MODIFY REPORT command clause.

The parameters element is ignored if you do not specify a DataEnvironment class or if _frxcommand discovers that your DataEnvironment object does not derive from _deabstract or implement a similar API. If your DataEnvironment object matches this API, _frxcommand closes tables if it had opened them previously. _Frxcommand then "feeds" the DataEnvironment a set of SelectCmd specifications to be added to each SQL statement, as a WHERE clause, allowing you to indicate complicated query filters and conditions at runtime.

To use the parameters element, simply include attributes on the element with names that match your cursor aliases for the DataEnvironment class. Use the query condition as the value of each attribute, without preceding it by the keyword "WHERE". For example:

```
<newworld5.frx>
<print>prompt</print>
<preview/>
<parameters country="Name LIKE '%anistan'"
city="population &gt; 130000"/>
</newworld5.frx>
```

_Deabstract matches your attribute names with the aliases available in its collection, and adjusts each SelectCmd before executing each query. Attributes for which no appropriate cursor is available, based on the alias, are ignored.

> *Notice that I used* **>** *, encoding the > sign, in the attribute value, to avoid any issues with the use of a control character within an attribute value in the XML document. Strictly speaking, you don't need to do this with the > sign. However the < character must always be encoded as* **<** *within an attribute value according to the XML standard. I always do both, to avoid confusion.*

The parameters element makes it possible for you to supply free-form, complex filter statements while still allowing you to maintain close control over your SQL statement at runtime.

> *To avoid SQL injection attacks while leveraging the power and freedom this feature allows, do not provide an interface that lets users type this clause in directly in the form of a WHERE clause.*

> *Provide user interface elements that specify values for various fields, such as you see in Figure 88, and construct the resulting WHERE clause in your code. Admittedly, the interface in Figure 88 is not beautiful; I am not much of a Web interface designer. Also, it is tedious to design and manage this type of interface rather than one large editbox in which experienced users can type SQL directly. However, it is a much safer practice.*

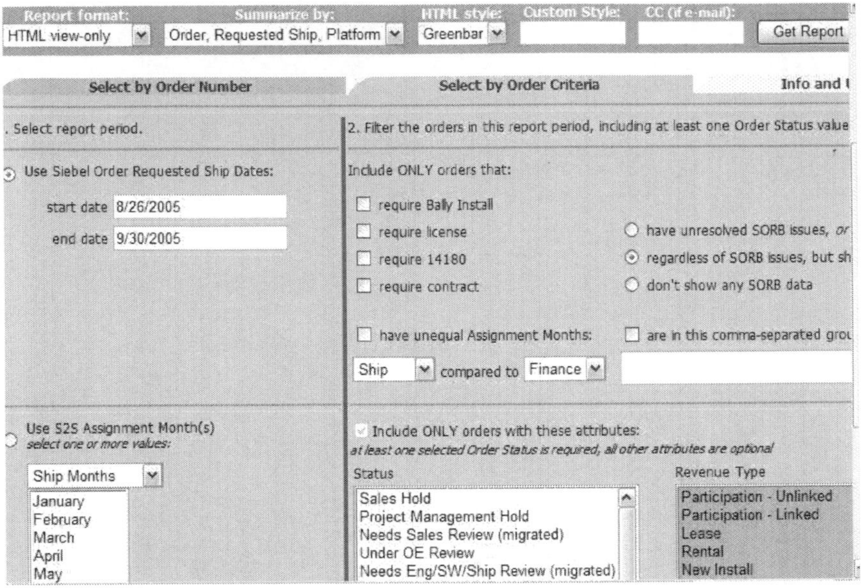

Figure 88. A report querying interface does not have to be beautiful, but it should give users varied and explicit choices. You can translate extensive choices into parameters for output and pass them to _FrxCommand.

The test xml files in your "deploy" folder include the NEWWORLD5.FRX example you see in the listing above, as the contents of the file testPrintPromptParameters.xml.

In this code, you also see child elements of the report action node specifying both print and preview activities, with the print element including a prompt keyword. This usage is documented fully in the schema file.

The additional test xml files in your "deploy" folder give you working examples of design actions and other types of actions implemented by _frxcommand's request schema.

For example, testPreview specifies two different reports chained together in a preview, and also features use of the range clause of the REPORT FORM command and the root attribute TopForm:

```
<root DEClass="NewWorld_NoAuto" DEOpenTables="1"
DEClassLib="WorldData" TopForm="1" >

<newworld5.frx>

<preview></preview>

<continued/><range>1</range>

</newworld5.frx>
```

```
<unrelated_world.frx><preview/><range>9,10</range>
</unrelated_world.frx>

</root>
```

As you see above, this file uses the special _frxcommand keyword continued on the first report. To _fxcommand, this keyword implies the NOWAIT and NOPAGEEJECT keywords of the REPORT FORM command when your XML instructions also include the preview node. In other words, if _frxcommand is constructing a REPORT or LABEL FORM command, and it sees its continued keyword, it includes the NOPAGEEJECT keyword on the command. If the command also includes PREVIEW, it adds NOPAGEEJECT as well. The continued element can be used instead of NOPAGEEJECT for other types of output, such as PRINT and HTML; _frxcommand adds the NOPAGEEJECT for any type of non-design action.

The schema supports the use of nopageeject and nowait instead, if you prefer, with nowait being ignored if the action is not a preview. Either version works only to "chain" output of the same type (for example, two previews or two HTML results).

> *You must be careful to use neither* **continued** *nor* **nopageeject** *on the last report in a series of instructions. As explained in the VFP documentation, NOPAGEEJECT indicates that the output queue (such as a file handle for the HTML or a print job for printing) should not be closed. The last report in a series must always close the queue.*

The testHtml.XML file is an example of using VFP 9's extension output types, which uses the OBJECT <objectreference> or OBJECT TYPE <N> clause. _Frxcommand supports extension output through its TYPE <N> variant; that is, you have to specify a known type by number. (VFP 9.0 supports types 4 (XML) and 5 (HTML) out-of-the-box). You can also use this syntax to support the native output types; use type 0 for print and type 1 for preview. When you use this syntax you automatically specify object-assisted versions of all output.

The report action node contains a child element, objectType, to support this clause of the native command. The schema type definition for this portion of the request XML schema is shown in Figure 89. Typically, extension output generates a file so, although you see that the schema indicates the fileName attribute is optional, you almost always want to specify this value along with the required type attribute, which indicates the OBJECT TYPE clause's required numeric value.

The extensionAttributes child node for the objecttype element provides a way to set any property belonging to the ReportListener base class, or that a developer may add to a ReportListener-derived output class. As indicated by the annotations you'll find in the schema, _frxcommand attempts to cast your specified values to an appropriate VFP type, using the type attribute before assigning the value attribute to each member property you specify by name in your extension instructions.

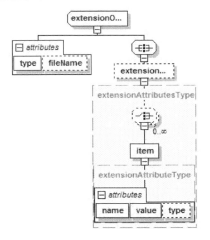

Figure 89. The objecttype child node for a report request element.

In testHtml.XML, I've used the extensionAttributes feature to specify a print-JobName value for the associated reportListener.

```
<root QuietMode="1">
<unrelated_world.frx>
<objectType type="5"
fileName=".\test.html"><range>1</range>
<extensionAttributes>
<item name="printJobName" value="My HTML Report"
type="C"/>
</extensionAttributes>
</objectType>
</unrelated_world.frx>
</root>
```

When the objectType element's type attribute value is 0, indicating a print run, the native ReportListener class uses its printJobName attribute to specify the name of the print job as it appeared in the Windows print queue manager window. When the type value is 1, the default preview application also "understands" the printjobname attribute, and applies it to the preview title bar. The HtmlListener class "understands" this attribute to be applicable to the title element of the HTML, as you see when you try the XML instructions; the resulting TEST.HTML file displays in Figure 90.

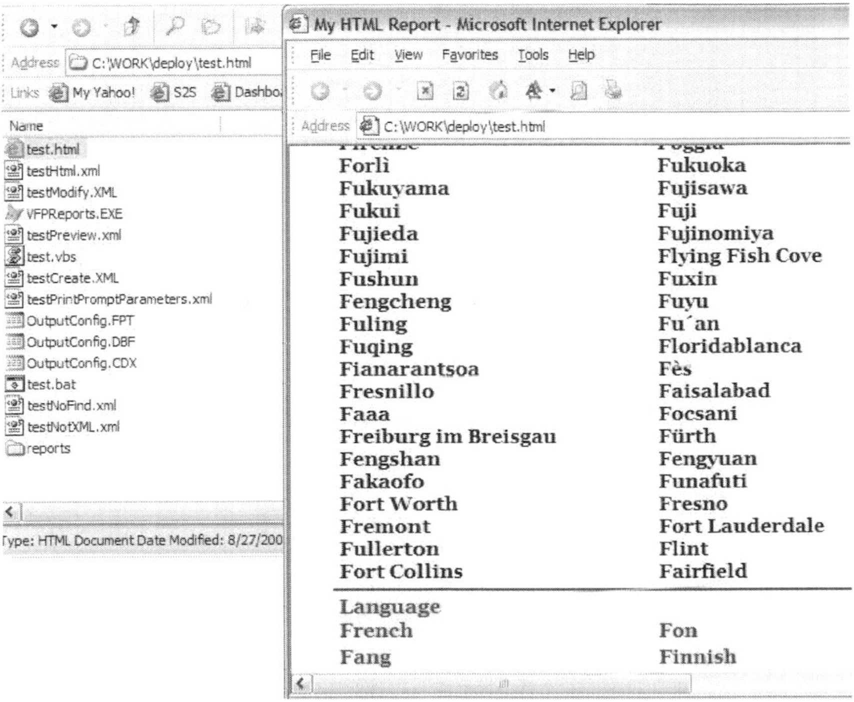

Figure 90. HTML Results in the "deploy" folder and browser window.

> *In Figure 90, you also see some additional generated files after running testHtml.XML: OutputConfig.DBF, with its associated CDX and FPT files. This is a lookup table for several of the file-based extension-output types; you can ignore it. The file size will not grow after these (small) files are initially created. If you prefer, you can build the lookup table into your VFPREPORTS and VFPREPORTSCOM projects. Refer to the VFP documentation for more information.*

7.5 Providing end-user design sessions using _frxcommand and PROTECTED reports

The testCreate.XML and testModify.XML files show you how _frxcommand works when you choose to provide a design session, rather than a report run, for your end-users. As shown here, testModify.XML features the use of the protected instruction, along with my standard practice of opening the tables for a design session before beginning to modify the report:

```
<root DEClass="deworld" DEOpenTables="1"
DEClassLib="WorldData" TopForm="1" >

<world_with_class.frx design="0" >

<protected/>

</world_with_class.frx>

<world_with_class.frx >

<preview/>

</world_with_class.frx>

</root>
```

If you use this instruction, whether by using _frxcommand or by including the PROTECTED clause on a MODIFY REPORT statement in the IDE , there are some changes immediately evident in the design session. The **Protection** tab of Report Builder dialogs -- first seen in the Multiple Selection and Report Properties dialogs in Figures 39 and 40 – are unavailable. However, the real power of the protection feature is not evident until you actually add protection instructions to an FRX, by making choices from the **Protection** tabs available in various Report Builder dialogs.

I have edited the version of WORLD_WITH_CLASS.FRX in your "deploy" files to include appropriate protection changes.

> *In your applications you don't have to maintain a special, protected version of your reports for deployment purposes; simply edit without the PROTECTED clause in your developer/IDE sessions and deploy the same FRX, adding the keyword for your end-users' sessions. I have changed only the "deploy" copy of this report so you can modify both copies with the PROTECTED clause, to see the difference my choices make.*

The schema specifies that you add protection instructions as a child element of a report action node, not a simple attribute. Although it currently has no attributes or qualifying behavior, it is possible to imagine reporting extensions that issue complex protection instructions dynamically at runtime, including user security and access levels to different protection features.

Figure 91 shows you some global protection settings I highly recommend for reports deployed with _frxcommand, including limiting access to complex report features such as variables and (especially) the Data Environment.

For design use with _frxcommand, you may also want to eliminate previewing ability, as shown in the figure. _Frxcommand must force old-style preview when previewing from the Designer, at least in the current version. You can always follow a design action with a preview of the same report in the _frxcommand instructions (as I've done in testModify.xml).

> You notice that I've included the global attribute *TopForm* in *testModify.XML*, but _frxcommand forces the Report Designer into Screen. In this version, _frxcommand does not support Designer sessions in top forms. The *TopForm* attribute is included to support the subsequent preview action. (Future versions may support Designer in top form mode as well.)

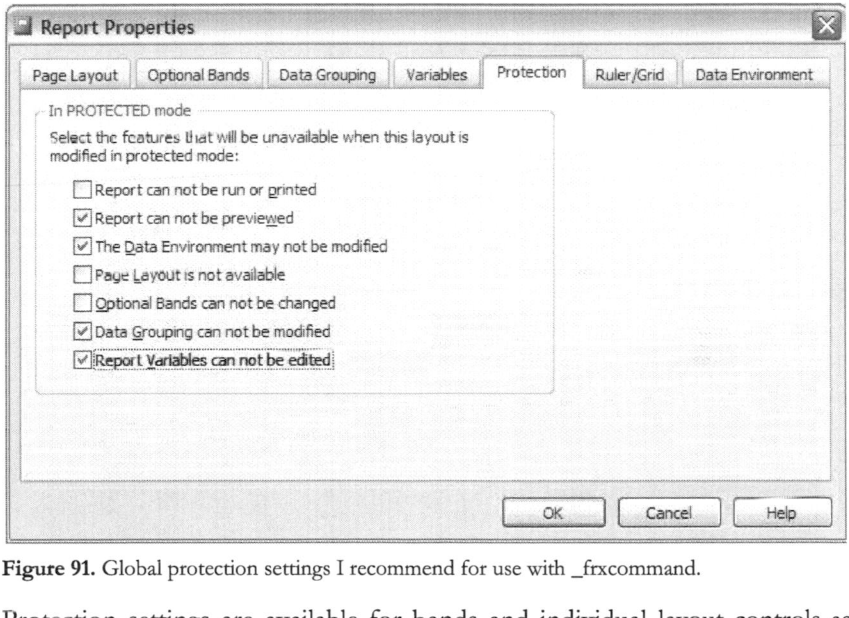

Figure 91. Global protection settings I recommend for use with _frxcommand.

Protection settings are available for bands and individual layout controls as well as globally. In the "deploy" version of WORLD_WITH_CLASS.FRX, I've eliminated access to the Properties dialog for all bands except a few of the footers, using the Band Properties dialog instructions you see in Figure 92.

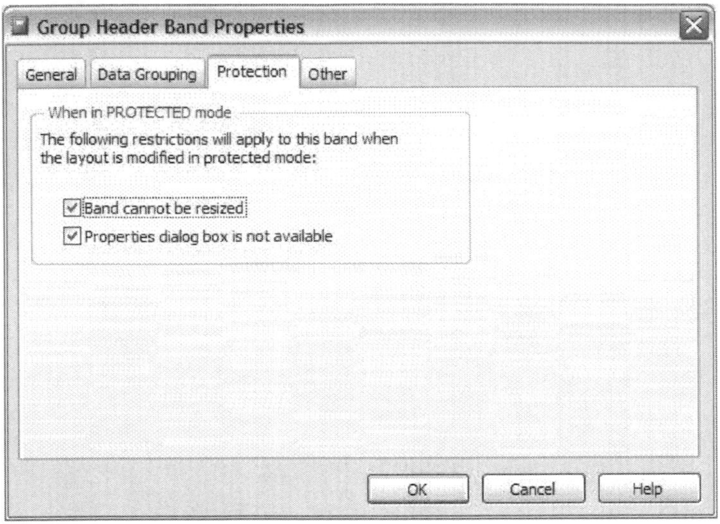

Figure 92. Band protection selections.

On an individual layout control level, protection options are extensive (see Figure 93); you can even specify that a report layout control does not appear in the design layout at all!

But your object-level customization features don't stop there. In Figure 93, you can see that I've specified a "Design-Time Caption" to appear in the protected report layout instead of the complex underlying expression (**ALLTR(Country.name)** + **"** (**"** + **ALLTR(Country.Uname)** + **")"**). If I choose to allow access to the Properties dialog for this layout control in protected mode, the user still has access to the original expression, but the design layout presents a "friendly" alternative.

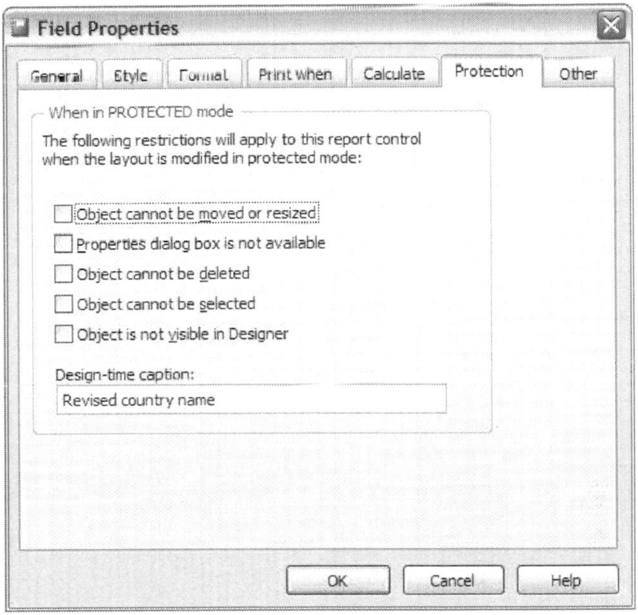

Figure 93. Layout control protection.

You can see the result in Figure 94. This screen shot of the WORLD_WITH_CLASS being edited using the testModify.XML instructions also shows you a tooltip for the country name layout control.

Tooltips are available both in PROTECTED and standard design modes. You create them on the **Other** tab of the various Report Builder properties dialogs, shown in Figure 95. Note that, in a PROTECTED design session, this tab shows only the **Comments** entry to end-users.

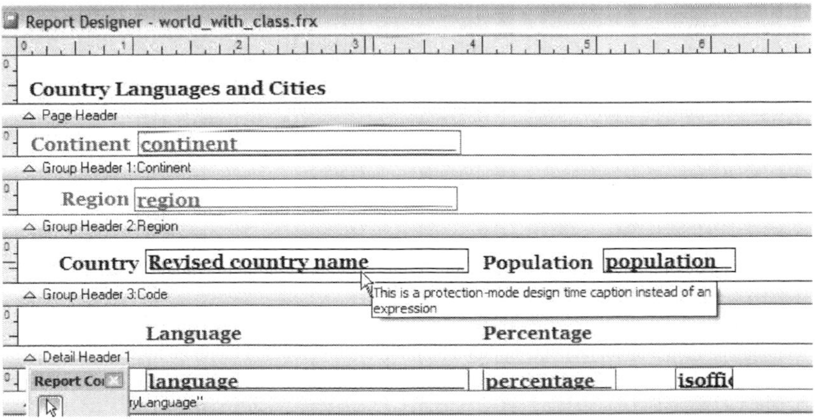

Figure 94. A protected layout in a design session shows a design-time caption and a tooltip.

Figure 95. The "Other" tab in a properties dialog, where you create tooltips (shown in standard, not PROTECTED, design mode).

7.6 Extending _frxcommand

Although, as I explained earlier, you do not need to derive customized classes from _frxcommand to use it, this class is not "sealed" (in dotNet syntax) or "final" (in java syntax). In other words, if you want to extend the class, you are allowed to do so, and _frxcommand comes equipped with some special hooks in areas that will repay your effort.

I've added the items I recommend you investigate to the _frxcommand class's **Favorites** tab, shown in Figure 96.

In the figure, you notice the logFeedback method discussed earlier, as well as the findListenerForType method highlighted in the Properties window. You could augment this method to add more extension output types you wanted to support in your application (binding the appropriate class library into your application, of course).

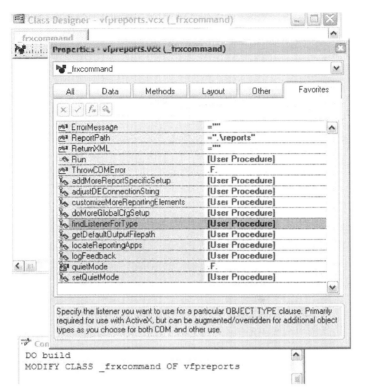

Figure 96. Some properties and methods recommended for investigation in the _frxcommand class.

The **Favorites** tab also shows you several "hook" methods designed to let you customize the report listeners used for various standard output types, adjust the global setup for the report run, or adjust the report-action setup for a specific run.

For example, when _frxcommand configures the DataEnvironment object, you can use the adjustDEConnectionString method to change its behavior at runtime. This method receives the DEConnectionString you specified in the XML, and it can either entirely replace this value or use it to decrypt or otherwise adjust the XML value before returning the correct run-time value for processing.

If you generate the XML instructions on the fly, and supply them to _frxcommand as a string or erase the XML file after the run, you may not need this capability. However, this feature gives you a chance to protect your server and access information even further.

One good mechanism would be to store a skeleton of the appropriate connection string directly in your XML, or directly in the _deabstract-derived class's connectionString property value, like this:

DRIVER=XXX;SERVER=YYY;DATABASE=world;USER=AA; PASSWORD=BB;OPTIONS=3;

Now the adjustDEConnectionString method can do something like the following:

```
LPARAMETERS tvValue

LOCAL lcReturnValue = TRANSFORM(tvValue)

lcReturnValue = STRTRAN(lcReturnValue,;
"XXX",THIS.GetInfo("driver"))

lcReturnValue = STRTRAN(lcReturnValue, "YYY",;
THIS.GetInfo("server"))

lcReturnValue = STRTRAN(lcReturnValue, "AA",;
THIS.GetInfo("user"))

lcReturnValue = STRTRAN(lcReturnValue, "BB",;
THIS.GetInfo("password"))

RETURN lcReturnValue
```

The code above uses a GetInfo(<key>) method you would add to the _frxcommand class. It receives the proper value for each item from GetInfo and substitutes appropriate values in the connection string skeleton, one at a time.

Where should the proposed GetInfo method get the proper information for each substitution? This method can read and translate encrypted values from a file in a protected location or follow whatever strategy you prefer.

As a simple alternative, you can use the Project Info settings for your VFPREPORTS and VFPREPORTSCOM projects to set encryption for your EXE and DLL files. You can see this dialog in Figure 97. (I recommend you do this for deployment purposes in any application, along with removing debugging information from the production versions, as shown in the figure.)

Once you have done this, you'll find the strings you add to DEFINES.PRG as constants values are not visible if you examine the EXE and DLL in a text editor, so you could add #DEFINEd constants for each element of the connection string.

Although the project build encryption is not unbreakable, it adds a layer of obfuscation at very low cost. As a drawback, the information in these constants is not easily adjusted at runtime, as you know; once you've built the application, you would have to re-build it to change the access and server information. However, you could use a combination approach here: use a #DEFINEd constant to read the protected location and filename from which you read your connection information. You could then adjust the information in this file without re-building or re-distributing the application file.

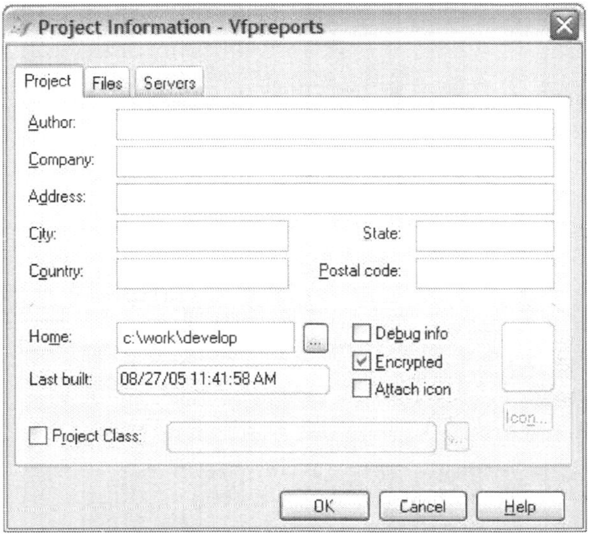

Figure 97. The Project Options dialog, with some recommended settings for deployed applications. Fill out the other items here to suit your needs!

Because this capability (adjusting connection strings) is quite important, and because you might use _deabstract and related strategies without using _frxcommand, you'll find that _deabstract offers a similar capability or hook: a protected setConnectionString method of the _deabstract, invoked during initialization of the class, allows you to specify the class' connectionString property value on the fly.

You can choose to write your extension code to your derived DataEnvironment classes, rather than _frxcommand, and follow any of the general strategies discussed above to obtain the correct values at runtime

7.7 Building a distributable VFP reporting solution

Now that you know how to build, test, and use your executable application and ActiveX objects, you need to know how to deploy these items, as well as associated VFP requirements such as runtime files, to your client's installation.

Most of the actions you take in this part of the development process are well-covered in the VFP 9 help file. In this section, I highlight those sections of the help file, and of the process, that are of special concern in report-centric applications.

VFP 9 ships with a specially-branded version of InstallShield (the Install-Shield Express Visual FoxPro Limited Edition). You can use it to create a SETUP.EXE, to install and configure all the necessary files.

As noted at the beginning of this tutorial, this component is optional when you install VFP. You can substitute other mechanisms for the steps I supply here, as long as they complete the same tasks.

VFP 9's help file includes an excellent "Walkthrough" topic, **Walkthrough: Creating a Visual FoxPro Application Setup Program Using Install-Shield**, describing the full process of creating a SETUP.EXE with this version of InstallShield. I highly recommend you read and follow the steps in this walkthrough.

There are a number of required MSMs (merge modules) required to support a Visual FoxPro general installation; these are listed in the Walkthrough. You find these in the **Redistributables** panel of InstallShield, shown with a red "check mark" in Figure 99 below. I recommend you ensure the availability of the latest version of MDAC (Microsoft Data Access Components) as one of the MSMs you include in every installation.

You notice that there are some special instructions for use in report-centric applications:

You should also include the Microsoft Visual FoxPro 9 Report Applications merge module which contains runtime applications used by the Visual FoxPro 9.0 reporting engine. For more information, see Including Report Files for Distribution.

The linked topic mentioned above, shown in Figure 98, lists the MSMs which are optional for some VFP applications, but which are required for the kinds of reporting applications described in this tutorial. Ensure that your Setup project includes all the MSM files shown in this list.

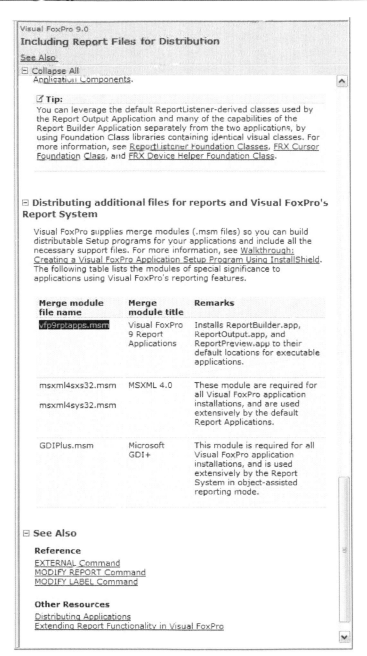

Figure 98. The help file's **Including Report Files for Distribution** topic lists merge modules you need to include in your Setup.

Figure 99 shows you the **ODBC Resources** panel in InstallShield. As you can see, I've selected the MySQL driver to be included in my installation. If you have multiple driver versions, select the version with which you have tested your application and which you plan to use in your connection string property values.

If you are following the strategy I've recommended in this tutorial, you do not have to include any DSNs (ODBC setups) that you may have created on your development machine. Notice, in Figure 99, that I have not selected the DSN I created for convenience during development.

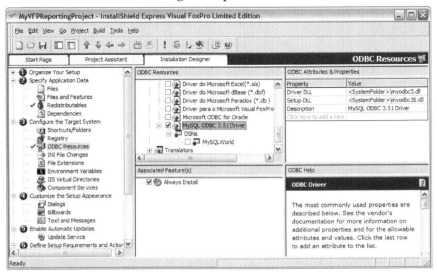

Figure 99. Editing **ODBC Resources** information in InstallShield.

For the Application Files section, you must include the VFPREPORTS.EXE and, if you're using ActiveX in the DLL version, include the VFPREPORTSCOM.DLL as well.

I usually include the small VBR and TLB files, generated by the project build process, which you see in Figure 100, although they may not be necessary. These provide some extra information that may be useful for any applications on the target system that use object browsers or that participate in the registration process in Windows.

You also add your FRX/FRX files to the distribution. As shown in Figure 100, I've placed these files in a separate folder under the installation directory of the EXE and DLL files. This is the default place that _frxcommand uses to find your reports although, as you know you can configure the XML instructions with other locations, using the ReportPath global attribute. You can set the reports directory (whatever its name) to be installed as part of an Optional application feature in InstallShield, and also mark the FRX and FRT as Shared in their Properties dialogs. Adjust your XML command files to point to the shared location, and install the FRX and FRTs only once for all users.

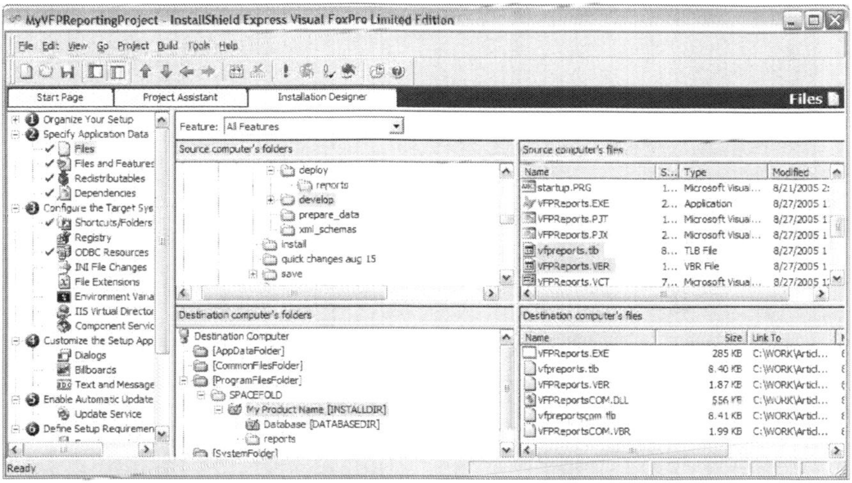

Figure 100. Selecting your application files.

To ensure availability of the ActiveX server objects on the target computer, rightclick on each destination file containing a server object (the EXE and DLL), and choose the **COM & .NET Settings** tab from its Properties dialog. Select **Extract COM Information** as its **Registration type**, as shown in Figure 101 and as recommended by the help file.

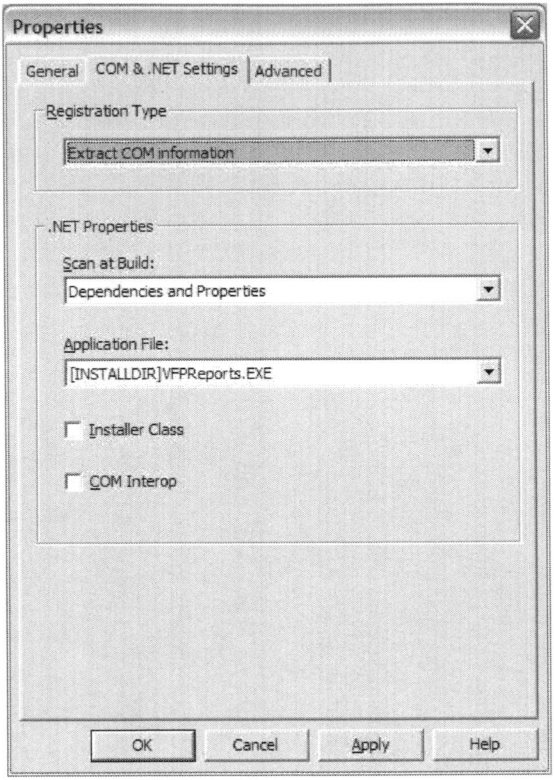

Figure 101. Set COM registration properties for the EXE and DLL destination files.

The VFP9RPTAPPS.MSM file (highlighted in the help file topic in Figure 98) installs three VFP reporting components (REPORTOUTPUT.APP, REPORTBUILDER.APP, and REPORTPREVIEW.APP) to their default location. If you prefer, you can install these three files to your program file main directory, which allows you to maintain separate versions of these applications in case multiple VFP applications exist on the computer. Simply pull the three *.APP files from your VFP development installation directory.

You can also replace these files with branded or enhanced versions, or even build the components directly into your EXE and DLL files, rather than distributing them separately. Full instructions are included in the help file topic shown in the figure (**Including Report Files for Distribution**).

Should you choose to use non-default Report Application components, as explained in the help file, you must tell your application where to find your replacement files for each of the reporting application components. If you remember, your two projects include a special text file: CONFIG.FPW, that allows you to specify these files' locations and other relevant settings. You can see this file, open as a text file, in Figure 102.

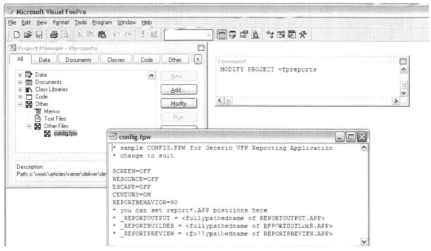

Figure 102. Editing CONFIG.FPW.

The CONFIG.FPW file built into your EXE and DLL can also replicate many of the environment settings you may have specified while working with VFP in development. For example, you remember the CENTURY setting you adjusted while setting up your IDE, before beginning work. To set the same environment in a distributed application, you can add instructions to the CONFIG.FPW.

As a general rule, any setting you provided in the Tools Options dialog is also available as a SET <something> command from the Command Window, and any SET command is available from the CONFIG.FPW as a <name>=<setting> statement. Refer to the help file for full details.

> *You can include the switch ALLOWEXTERNAL=ON in your built-in CONFIG.FPW if you would like to override some of these settings in the distributed application. You can then add an external CONFIG.FPW on disk in your setup project. However, this setting only works for command-line use of VFPREPORTS.EXE, not for the ActiveX server objects.*

7.8 Some ideas and thoughts about invoking your VFP component in external applications

If you've included all the files recommended above, you can build and deploy your SETUP.EXE successfully on a client computer. You may want to include some test XML files in your setup, similar to the ones I've included in the "deploy" directory, to verify installation, but that's about it. You can add more FRX files to the target site, as you continue to work with your data, later on. You don't need to build them all into a revised setup.

As you've already seen, you can call the ActiveX component or the VFPREPORTS executable from an external application, so, aside from determining exactly what instructions you should put in your XML command files for a given application, you're ready to go.

If, however, you are a MySQL developer, you may have some concerns about calling a VFP ActiveX control from your PHP application that I have not answered here. You may have to learn about the PHP-specific syntax appropriate to the use of COM or DCOM (which requires the **com.allow_dcom** switch in your PHP.INI) before achieving your desired result.

If you are a Java programmer, you may need to research using the term "java-com bridge" before you can use the ActiveX component successfully.

If you are a DotNet programmer, you know that you must manage the joys of COM-InterOp to do the same thing.

Clarifying every aspect of using ActiveX controls from all these environments is outside the scope of this paper, and accessing a VFP ActiveX control isn't very different from other COM-based objects you may have used. However, I do want to address two areas that might be of specific concern to MySQL developers, with specific implications for a report-centric application: considerations for use from a non-Wintel PHP or Java installation, and considerations for use from a web server. These two areas are significant, and often combined.

Although in some cases you can fulfill such requirements using ActiveX, your potential use of MySQL from (for example) a Linux web server was the real reason I included the EXE's command-line syntax in the VFPREPORTS architecture. If you want to allow design sessions, and other "visible" components of VFPREPORTS, such as previewing, the user must be on a VFP-capable machine – and that means Wintel-based. For a web server or other report content server, however, you just need file or print output, and you should be able to do this from a non-Wintel computer if desired.

If your web server is on a *Nix-platform box, you can invoke the VFP executable on a separate machine. You can use the Windows Remote Shell Service or the Interix Remote Shell Daemon (rshd) both of which are supplied with Windows Services for Unix. There are a number of freeware alternative versions of both rsh and ssh/scp for Windows.

From a security standpoint, you should note that the only part of the "conversation" between these two computers for which you might need security would be the file transfer (the transfer of either a batch file or a command xml file to the Windows machine, and the transfer of either the string results or the html/xml file back to the web server). Executing the EXE with its argument is not an inherently insecure operation unless you include the access information (server, username, and password) directly in the XML and supply the XML as a string argument rather than a filename. Beyond security issues, this technique is not practical for long and complex XML command instructions, in any case.

From a configuration standpoint, I want to point out that you need at least one default printer setup available on the machine hosting VFP, even if you're generating HTML only. VFP's report engine requires a print setup to get some idea of page size, when running any report.

If you want HTML or XML output, use the objecttype node, as described earlier in this document. The VFP Reporting XML schema output format is exhaustively documented in the help file, and the default HTML output or any other XML-based output can be produced using the XSLT facilities included in classes generating this output.

If you would like to create PDF documents for your web server output, I recommend you set up a PostScript printer driver and make it available to the executing machine (can be local printer or network) and use the PrinterName attribute (global) or printerName attribute (report-specific) to specify this printer. Use file node on the report action element to indicate the name of the resulting postscript file. Pipe the results through GhostScript on the web server, either using separate PS files or one continued file for multiple reports according to your needs. Because this is a common practice on *Nix systems, I will not go into details about it here.